CALVIN ON EPHESIANS

By John Calvin

ISBN: 9781520988979

April 2017

CW01086659

John Calvin's Ephesians Commentary Contents

CALVIN: EPHESIANS INTRODUCTION

THE ARGUMENT

Ephesus, which is familiarly known in history under a great variety of names, (106) was a very celebrated city of Lesser Asia. The remarkable events connected with the work of God in "forming there a people for himself," (Isaiah 43:21,) through the labors of Paul, together with the commencement and progress of that church, are related by Luke in the Acts of the Apostles. At present, I shall do nothing more than glance at what bears directly on the argument of the Epistle. The Ephesians had been instructed by Paul in the pure doctrine of the gospel. At a later period, while he was a prisoner at Rome, and perceiving that they needed confirmation, he wrote to them, on that account, the present Epistle.

The first three chapters are chiefly occupied with commending the grace of God. Immediately after the salutation in the commencement of the first chapter, he treats of God's free election. This affords him an opportunity of stating that they were now called into the kingdom of God, because they had been appointed to life before they were born. And here occurs a striking display of God's wonderful mercy, when the salvation of men is traced to its true and native source, the free act of adoption. But as the minds of men are ill fitted to receive so sublime a mystery, he betakes himself to prayer, that God would enlighten the Ephesians in the full knowledge of Christ.

In the second chapter, by drawing two comparisons, he places in a strong light the riches of divine grace. 1.He reminds them how wretched they were before they were called to Christ. We never become duly sensible of our obligations to Christ, nor estimate aright his kindness towards us, till we have been led to view, on the other side, the unhappy condition in which we formerly were "without Christ." (Ephesians 2:12.) 2.The Gentiles were "aliens" from the promises of eternal life, which God had been pleased to bestow on the Jews alone.

In the third chapter, he declares that he had been appointed to be, in a peculiar manner, the Apostle of the Gentiles, because, for a long period, they were "strangers and foreigners," (Ephesians 2:19,) but are now included among the people of God. As this was an unusual event, and as its very novelty produced uneasiness in many minds, he calls it a

"mystery which in other ages was not made known
to the sons of men," (Ephesians 3:4,)

but "the dispensation" (Ephesians 3:2) of which had been intrusted to himself.

Towards the close of the chapter, he again prays that God would grant to the Ephesians such an intimate knowledge of Christ, that they would have no desire to know anything else. His object in doing so is not merely to lead them to gratitude to God for so many favors, and to the expression of that gratitude by entire devotion to his service, but still more to remove all doubt about his own calling. Paul was probably afraid that the false apostles would shake their faith by insinuating that they had been only half-instructed. They had been Gentiles, and, when they embraced pure Christianity, had been told nothing about ceremonies or circumcision. But all who enjoined on Christians the observance of the law were loud in the avowal, that those who have not been introduced into the church of God by circumcision must be held as profane persons. This was their ordinary song, that no man who is not circumcised is entitled to be reckoned among the people of God, and that all the rites prescribed by Moses ought to be observed. Accordingly, they brought it as a charge against Paul, that he exhibited Christ as equally the Savior of Gentiles and of Jews. They asserted that his apostleship was a profanation of the heavenly doctrine, because it threw open to wicked men, without discrimination, a share in the covenant of grace.

That the Ephesians, when assailed by these calumnies, might not give way, he resolved to meet them. While he argues so earnestly that they were called to the gospel because they had been chosen before the creation of the world, he charges them, on the other hand, not to imagine that the gospel had been accidentally brought to them by the will of men, or that it flew to them by chance; (107) for the preaching of Christ among them was nothing else than the announcement of that eternal decree. While he lays before them the unhappy condition of their former life, he at the same time reminds them that the singular and astonishing mercy of God appeared in rescuing them from so deep a gulf. While he sets before their eyes his own commission as the apostle of the Gentiles, he confirms them in the faith which they had once received, because they had been divinely admitted into the communion of the church. And yet each of the sentences to which we have now referred must be viewed as an exhortation fitted to excite the Ephesians to gratitude.

In the fourth chapter, he describes the manner in which the Lord governs and protects his church, which is, by the gospel preached by men. Hence it follows, that in no other way can its integrity be preserved, and that the object at which it aims is true perfection. The apostle's design is, to commend to the Ephesians the ministry by which God reigns amongst us. He afterwards details the fruits of this preaching, — a holy life and all the duties of piety. Nor does he satisfy himself with describing in general terms how Christians ought to live, but lays down particular exhortations adapted to the various relations of society.

CALVIN EPHESIANS 1

Verse 1

Paul, an apostle. As the same form of salutation, or at least very little varied, is found in all the Epistles, it would be superfluous to repeat here the observations which we have formerly made. He calls himself "an apostle of Jesus Christ;" for all to whom has been given the ministry of reconciliation are his ambassadors. The word Apostle, indeed, carries something more; for it is not every minister of the gospel, as we shall afterwards see, (Ephesians 4:11,) that can be called an apostle. But this subject has been explained more fully in my remarks on the Epistle to the Galatians. (See Calvin on "Galatians 1:1 ")

He adds, by the will of God; for "no man ought to take this honor unto himself," (Hebrews 5:4,) but every man ought to wait for the calling of God, which alone makes lawful ministers. He thus meets the jeers of wicked men by holding out the authority of God, and removes every occasion of inconsiderate strife.

To all the saints. He gives the name of saints to those whom he afterwards denominates faithful in Christ Jesus. No man, therefore, is a believer who is not also a saint; and, on the other hand, no man is a saint who is not a believer. Most of the Greek copies want the word all; but I was unwilling to strike it out, because it must, at all events, be understood.

Verse 3

Blessed (108) be the God and Father of our Lord Jesus Christ. The lofty terms in which he extolls the grace of God toward the Ephesians, are intended to rouse their hearts to gratitude, to set them all on flame, to fill them even to overflowing with this thought. They who perceive in themselves discoveries of the Divine goodness, so full and absolutely perfect, and who make them the subject of earnest meditation, will never embrace new doctrines, by which the very grace which they feel so powerfully in themselves is thrown into the shade. The design of the apostle, therefore, in asserting the riches of divine grace toward the Ephesians, was to protect them against having their faith shaken by the false apostles, as if their calling were doubtful, or salvation were to be sought in some other way. He shews, at the same time, that the full certainty of future happiness rests on the revelation of his love to us in Christ, which God makes in the gospel. But to confirm the matter more fully, he rises to the first cause, to the fountain, — the eternal election of God, by which, ere we are born, (Romans 9:11,) we are adopted as sons. This makes it evident that their salvation was accomplished, not by any accidental or unlooked-for occurrence, but by the eternal and unchangeable decree of God.

The word bless is here used in more than one sense, as referring to God, and as referring to men. I find in Scripture four different significations of this word.1.We are said to bless God when we offer praise to him for his goodness.2.God is said to bless us, when he crowns our undertakings with success, and, in the exercise of his goodness, bestows upon us happiness and prosperity; and the reason is, that our enjoyments depend entirely upon his pleasure. Our attention is here called to the singular efficacy which dwells in the very word of God, and which Paul expresses in beautiful language.3.Men bless each other by prayer.4.The priest's blessing is not simply a prayer, but is likewise a testimony and pledge of the Divine blessing; for the priests received a commission to bless in the name of the Lord. Paul therefore blesses God, because he hath blessed us, that is, hath enriched us with all blessing and grace.

With all spiritual blessings. I have no objection to Chrysostom's remark, that the word spiritual conveys an implied contrast between the blessing of Moses and of Christ. The law had its blessings; but in Christ only is perfection found, because he gives us a perfect revelation of the kingdom of God, which leads us directly to heaven. When the body itself is presented to us, figures are no longer needed.

In heavenly. Whether we understand the meaning to be, in heavenly Places, or in heavenly Benefits, is of little consequence. All that was intended to be expressed is the superiority of that grace which we receive through Christ. The happiness which it bestows is not in this world, but in heaven and everlasting life. In the Christian religion, indeed, as we are elsewhere taught, (1 Timothy 4:8,) is contained the "promise of the life that now is, and of that which is to come;" but its aim is spiritual happiness, for the kingdom of Christ is spiritual. A contrast is drawn between Christ and all the Jewish emblems, by which the blessing under the law was conveyed; for where Christ is, all those things are superfluous.

Verse 4

According as he hath chosen us. The foundation and first cause, both of our calling and of all the benefits which we receive from God, is here declared to be his eternal election. If the reason is asked, why God has called us to enjoy the gospel, why he daily bestows upon us so many blessings, why he opens to us the gate of heaven, — the answer will be constantly found in this principle, that he hath chosen us before the foundation of the world. The very time when the election took place proves it to be free; for what could we have deserved, or what merit did we possess, before the world was made? How childish is the attempt to meet this argument by the following sophism! "We were chosen because we were worthy, and because God foresaw that we would be worthy." We were all lost in Adam; and therefore, had not God, through

8

his own election, rescued us from perishing, there was nothing to be foreseen. The same argument is used in the Epistle to the Romans, where, speaking of Jacob and Esau, he says,

"For the children being not yet born, neither having done any good or evil, that the purpose of God according to election might stand, not of works, but of him that calleth." (Romans 9:11.)

But though they had not yet acted, might a sophist of the Sorbonne reply, God foresaw that they would act. This objection has no force when applied to the depraved natures of men, in whom nothing can be seen but materials for destruction.

In Christ. This is the second proof that the election is free; for if we are chosen in Christ, it is not of ourselves. It is not from a perception of anything that we deserve, but because our heavenly Father has introduced us, through the privilege of adoption, into the body of Christ. In short, the name of Christ excludes all merit, and everything which men have of their own; for when he says that we arechosen in Christ, it follows that in ourselves we are unworthy.

That we should be holy. This is the immediate, but not the chief design; for there is no absurdity in supposing that the same thing may gain two objects. The design of building is, that there should be a house. This is the immediate design, but the convenience of dwelling in it is the ultimate design. It was necessary to mention this in passing; for we shall immediately find that Paul mentions another design, the glory of God. But there is no contradiction here; for the glory of God is the highest end, to which our sanctification is subordinate.

This leads us to conclude, that holiness, purity, and every excellence that is found among men, are the fruit of election; so that once more Paul expressly puts aside every consideration of merit. If God had foreseen in us anything worthy of election, it would have been stated in language the very opposite of what is here employed, and which plainly means that all our holiness and purity of life flow from the election of God. How comes it then that some men are religious, and live in the fear of God, while others give themselves up without reserve to all manner of wickedness? If Paul may be believed, the only reason is, that the latter retain their natural disposition, and the former have been chosen to holiness. The cause, certainly, is not later than the effect. Election, therefore, does not depend on the righteousness of works, of which Paul here declares that it is the cause.

We learn also from these words, that election gives no occasion to licentiousness, or to the blasphemy of wicked men who say, "Let us live in any manner we please; for,

9

if we have been elected, we cannot perish." Paul tells them plainly, that they have no right to separate holiness of life from the grace of election; for

"whom he did predestinate, them he also called, and whom he called, them he also justified." (Romans 8:30.)

The inference, too, which the Catharists, Celestines, and Donatists drew from these words, that we may attain perfection in this life, is without foundation. This is the goal to which the whole course of our life must be directed, and we shall not reach it till we have finished our course. Where are the men who dread and avoid the doctrine of predestination as an inextricable labyrinth, who believe it to be useless and almost dangerous? No doctrine is more useful, provided it be handled in the proper and cautious manner, of which Paul gives us an example, when he presents it as an illustration of the infinite goodness of God, and employs it as an excitement to gratitude. This is the true fountain from which we must draw our knowledge of the divine mercy. If men should evade every other argument, election shuts their mouth, so that they dare not and cannot claim anything for themselves. But let us remember the purpose for which Paul reasons about predestination, lest, by reasoning with any other view, we fall into dangerous errors.

Before him it love. Holiness before God (κατενώπιον αὐτοῦ) is that of a pure conscience; for God is not deceived, as men are, by outward pretense, but looks to faith, or, which means the same thing, the truth of the heart. If we view the word love as applied to God, the meaning will be, that the only reason why he chose us, was his love to men. But I prefer connecting it with the latter part of the verse, as denoting that the perfection of believers consists in love; not that God requires love alone, but that it is an evidence of the fear of God, and of obedience to the whole law.

Verse 5

Who hath predestinated us. What follows is intended still further to heighten the commendation of divine grace. The reason why Paul inculcated so earnestly on the Ephesians the doctrines of free adoption through Christ, and of the eternal election which preceded it, has been already considered. But as the mercy of God is nowhere acknowledged in more elevated language, this passage will deserve our careful attention. Three causes of our salvation are here mentioned, and a fourth is shortly afterwards added. The efficient cause is the good pleasure of the will of God, the material cause is, Jesus Christ, and the final cause is, the praise of the glory of his grace. Let us now see what he says respecting each.

To the first belongs the whole of the following statement God hath predestinated us in himself, according to the good pleasure of his will, unto the adoption of sons, and hath made us accepted by his grace. In the word predestinate we must again attend to the order. We were not then in existence, and therefore there was no merit of ours. The cause of our salvation did not proceed from us, but from God alone. Yet Paul, not satisfied with these statements, adds in himself. The Greek phrase is , εἰς αὐτὸν, and has the same meaning with ἐν αὐτῷ. By this he means that God did not seek a cause out of himself, but predestinated us, because such was his will.

But this is made still more clear by what follows, according to the good pleasure of his will. The word will was enough, for Paul very frequently contrasts it with all outward causes by which men are apt to imagine that the mind of God is influenced. But that no doubt may remain, he employs the word good pleasure, which expressly sets aside all merit. In adopting us, therefore, God does not inquire what we are, and is not reconciled to us by any personal worth. His single motive is the eternal good pleasure, by which he predestinated us. (109) Why, then, are the sophists not ashamed to mingle with them other considerations, when Paul so strongly forbids us to look at anything else than the good pleasure of God?

Lest anything should still be wanting, he adds , ἐχαρίτωσεν ἐν χάριτι (110) This intimates, that, in the freest manner, and on no mercenary grounds, does God bestow upon us his love and favor, just as, when we were not yet born, and when he was prompted by nothing but his own will, he fixed upon us his choice. (111)

The material cause both of eternal election, and of the love which is now revealed, is Christ, the Beloved. This name is given, to remind us that by him the love of God is communicated to us. Thus he is the well-beloved, in order that we may be reconciled by him. The highest and last end is immediately added, the glorious praise of such abundant grace. Every man, therefore, who hides this glory, is endeavoring to overturn the everlasting purpose of God. Such is the doctrine of the sophists, which entirely overturns the doctrine of Christ, lest the whole glory of our salvation should be ascribed undividedly to God alone.

Verse 7

In whom we have redemption. The apostle is still illustrating the material cause, — the manner in which we are reconciled to God through Christ. By his death he has restored us to favor with the Father; and therefore we ought always to direct our minds to the blood of Christ, as the means by which we obtain divine grace. After

11

mentioning that, through the blood of Christ, we obtain redemption, he immediately styles it the forgiveness of sins, — to intimate that we are redeemed, because our sins are not imputed to us. Hence it follows, that we obtain by free grace that righteousness by which we are accepted of God, and freed from the chains of the devil and of death. The close connection which is here preserved, between our redemption itself and the manner in which it is obtained, deserves our notice; for, so long as we remain exposed to the judgment of God, we are bound by miserable chains, and therefore our exemption from guilt, becomes an invaluable freedom.

According to the riches of his grace. He now returns to the efficient cause, — the largeness of the divine kindness, which has given Christ to us as our Redeemer. Riches, and the corresponding word overflow, in the following verse, are intended to give us large views of divine grace. The apostle feels himself unable to celebrate, in a proper manner, the goodness of God, and desires that the contemplation of it would occupy the minds of men till they are entirely lost in admiration. How desirable is it that men were deeply impressed with "the riches of that grace" which is here commended! No place would any longer be found for pretended satisfactions, or for those trifles by which the world vainly imagines that it can redeem itself; as if the blood of Christ, when unsupported by additional aid, had lost all its efficacy. (112)

Verse 8

In all wisdom. He now comes to the formal cause, the preaching of the gospel, by which the goodness of God overflows upon us. (113) It is through faith that we receive Christ, by whom we come to God, and by whom we enjoy the privilege of adoption. Paul gives to the gospel the magnificent appellations of wisdom and prudence, for the purpose of leading the Ephesians to despise all contrary doctrines. The false apostles insinuated themselves, under the pretense of imparting views more elevated than the elementary instructions which Paul conveyed. And the devil, in order to undermine our faith, labors, as far as he can, to disparage the gospel. Paul, on the other hand, builds up the authority of the gospel, that believers may rest upon it with unshaken confidence. All wisdom means — full or perfect wisdom.

Verse 9

Having made known to us the mystery of his will. Some were alarmed at the novelty of his doctrine. With a view to such persons, he very properly denominates it a mystery of the divine will, and yet a mystery which God has now been pleased to reveal. As he formerly ascribed their election, so he now ascribes their calling, to the good pleasure of God. The Ephesians are thus led to consider that Christ has been made known, and the gospel preached to them, not because they deserved any such thing, but because it pleased God.

Which he hath purposed in himself. All is wisely and properly arranged. What can be more just than that his purposes, with which men are unacquainted, should be known to God alone, so long as he is pleased to conceal them, — or, again, that it should be in his own will and power to fix the time when they shall be communicated to men? The decree to adopt the Gentiles is declared to have been till now hidden in the mind of God, but so hidden, that God reserved it in his own power until the time of the revelation. Does any one now complain of it as a new and unprecedented occurrence, that those who were formerly "without God in the world," (Ephesians 2:12,) should be received into the church? Will he have the hardihood to deny that the knowledge of God is greater than that of men?

Verse 10

That in the dispensation of the fullness of times. That no man may inquire, why one time rather than another was selected, the apostle anticipates such curiosity, by calling the appointed period the fullness of times, the fit and proper season, as he also did in a former epistle. (Galatians 4:4) Let human presumption restrain itself, and, in judging of the succession of events, let it bow to the providence of God. The same lesson is taught by the word dispensation, for by the judgment of God the lawful administration of all events is regulated.

That he might gather together in one. In the old translation it is rendered (instaurare) restore; to which Erasmus has added (summatim) comprehensively. I have chosen to abide closely by the meaning of the Greek word , ἀνακεφαλαιώσασθαι, (114) because it is more agreeable to the context. The meaning appears to me to be, that out of Christ all things were disordered, and that through him they have been restored to order. And truly, out of Christ, what can we perceive in the world but mere ruins? We are alienated from God by sin, and how can we but present a broken and shattered aspect? The proper condition of creatures is to keep close to God. Such a gathering together (ἀνακεφαλαίωσις) as might bring us back to regular order, the apostle tells us, has been made in Christ. Formed into one body, we are united to God, and closely connected with each other. Without Christ, on the other hand, the whole world is a shapeless chaos and frightful confusion. We are brought into actual unity by Christ alone.

But why are heavenly beings included in the number? The angels were never separated from God, and cannot be said to have been scattered. Some explain it in this manner. Angels are said to be gathered together, because men have become members of the same society, are admitted equally with them to fellowship with God, and enjoy happiness in common with them by means of this blessed unity. The mode of expression is supposed to resemble one frequently used, when we speak of a whole building as repaired, many parts of which were ruinous or decayed, though some parts remained entire.

This is no doubt true; but what hinders us from saying that the angels also have been gathered together? Not that they were ever scattered, but their attachment to the service of God is now perfect, and their state is eternal. What comparison is there between a creature and the Creator, without the interposition of a Mediator? So far as they are creatures, had it not been for the benefit which they derived from Christ, they would have been liable to change and to sin, and consequently their happiness would not have been eternal. Who then will deny that both angels and men have been brought back to a fixed order by the grace of Christ? Men had been lost, and angels were not beyond the reach of danger. By gathering both into his own body, Christ hath united them to God the Father, and established actual harmony between heaven and earth.

Verse 11

Through whom also we have obtained an inheritance. Hitherto he has spoken generally of all the elect; he now begins to take notice of separate classes. When he says, WE have obtained, he speaks of himself and of the Jews, or, perhaps more correctly, of all who were the first fruits of Christianity; and afterwards he comes to the Ephesians. It tended not a little to confirm the faith of the Ephesian converts, that he associated them with himself and the other believers, who might be said to be the first-born in the church. As if he had said, "The condition of all godly persons is the same with yours; for we who were first called by God owe our acceptance to his eternal election." Thus, he shews, that, from first to last, all have obtained salvation by free grace, because they have been freely adopted according to eternal election.

Who worketh all things. The circumlocution employed in describing the Supreme Being deserves attention. He speaks of Him as the sole agent, and as doing everything according to His own will, so as to leave nothing to be done by man. In no respect, therefore, are men admitted to share in this praise, as if they brought anything of their own. God looks at nothing out of himself to move him to elect them, forthe counsel of his own will is the only and actual cause of their election. This may enable us to refute the error, or rather the madness, of those who, whenever they are unable to discover the reason of God's works, exclaim loudly against his design.

Verse 12

That we should be to the praise of his glory. Here again he mentions the final cause of salvation; for we must eventually become illustrations of the glory of God, if we are nothing but vessels of his mercy. The word glory, by way of eminence, (κατ '

ἐξοχὴν) denotes, in a peculiar manner, that which shines in the goodness of God; for there is nothing that is more peculiarly his own, or in which he desires more to be glorified, than goodness.

Verse 13

In whom ye also. He associates the Ephesians with himself, and with the rest of those who were the first fruits; for he says that they, in like manner, trusted in Christ. His object is, to shew that both had the same faith; and therefore we must supply the word trusted from the twelfth verse. He afterwards states that they were brought to that hope by the preaching of the gospel.

Two epithets are here applied to the gospel, — the word of truth, and the gospel of your salvation. Both deserve our careful attention. Nothing is more earnestly attempted by Satan than to lead us either to doubt or to despise the gospel. Paul therefore furnishes us with two shields, by which we may repel both temptations. In opposition to every doubt, let us learn to bring forward this testimony, that the gospel is not only certain truth, which cannot deceive, but is, by way of eminence, (κατ '

ἐξοχὴν,) the word of truth, as if, strictly speaking, there were no truth but itself. If the temptation be to contempt or dislike of the gospel, let us remember that its power and efficacy have been manifested in bringing to us salvation. The apostle had formerly declared that

"it is the power of God to salvation to every one that believeth," (Romans 1:16;)

but here he expresses more, for he reminds the Ephesians that, having been made partakers of salvation, they had learned this by their own experience. Unhappy they who weary themselves, as the world generally does, in wandering through many winding paths, neglecting the gospel, and pleasing themselves with wild romances, —

"ever learning and never able to come to the knowledge of the truth," (2 Timothy 3:7) or to find life! But happy they who have embraced the gospel, and whose attachment to it is steadfast; for this, beyond all doubt, is truth and life.

In whom also, after that ye believed. Having maintained that the gospel is certain, he now comes to the proof. And what higher surety can be found than the Holy Spirit? "Having denominated the gospel the word of truth, I will not prove it by the authority of men; for you have the testimony of the Spirit of God himself, who seals the truth of it in your hearts." This elegant comparison is taken from Seals, which among men have the effect of removing doubt. Seals give validity both to charters and to testaments; anciently, they were the principal means by which the writer of a letter could be known; and, in short, a seal distinguishes what is true and certain, from what is false and spurious. This office the apostle ascribes to the Holy Spirit, not only here, but in another part of this Epistle, (Ephesians 4:30,) and in the Second Epistle to the Corinthians, (2 Corinthians 1:22.) Our minds never become so firmly established in the truth of God as to resist all the temptations of Satan, until we have been confirmed in it by the Holy Spirit. The true conviction which believers have of the word of God, of their own salvation, and of religion in general, does not spring from the judgment of the flesh, or from human and philosophical arguments, but from the sealing of the Spirit, who imparts to their consciences such certainty as to remove all doubt. The foundation of faith would be frail and unsteady, if it rested on human wisdom; and therefore, as preaching is the instrument of faith, so the Holy Spirit makes preaching efficacious.

But is it not the faith itself which is here said to be sealed by the Holy Spirit? If so, faith goes before the sealing. I answer, there are two operations of the Spirit in faith, corresponding to the two parts of which faith consists, as it enlightens, and as it establishes the mind. The commencement of faith is knowledge: the completion of it is a firm and steady conviction, which admits of no opposing doubt. Both, I have said, are the work of the Spirit. No wonder, then, if Paul should declare that the Ephesians, who received by faith the truth of the gospel, were confirmed in that faith by the seal of the Holy Spirit.

With that Holy Spirit of promise. This title is derived from the effect produced; for to him we owe it that the promise of salvation is not made to us in vain. As God promises in his word, "that he will be to us a Father," (2 Corinthians 6:18,) so he gives to us the evidence of having adopted us by the Holy Spirit.

Verse 14

Which is the earnest (115) of our inheritance. This phrase is twice used by Paul in another Epistle. (2 Corinthians 1:22.) The metaphor is taken from bargains, in which, when a pledge has been given and accepted, the whole is confirmed, and no room is left for a change of mind. Thus, when we have received the Spirit of God, his promises are confirmed to us, and no dread is felt that they will be revoked. In themselves, indeed, the promises of God are not weak; but, until we are supported by the testimony of the Spirit, we never rest upon them with unshaken confidence. The Spirit, then, is the earnest of our inheritance of eternal life, until the redemption, that is, until the day of complete redemption is arrived. So long as we are in this world, our warfare is sustained by hope, and therefore this earnest is necessary; but when the possession itself shall have been obtained, the necessity and use of the earnest will then cease.

The significance of a pledge lasts no longer than till both parties have fulfilled the bargain; and, accordingly, he afterwards adds, ye are sealed to the day of redemption, (Ephesians 4:30,) which means the day of judgment. Though we are now redeemed by the blood of Christ, the fruit of that redemption does not yet appear; for "every creature groaneth, desiring to be delivered from the bondage of corruption. And not only they, but ourselves also, who have the first-fruits of the Spirit, even we ourselves groan within ourselves, waiting for the adoption, to wit, the redemption of our body;" for we have not yet obtained it, but by hope. (Romans 8:21.) But we shall obtain it in reality, when Christ shall appear to judgment. Such is the meaning of the word redemption in the passage now quoted from the Epistle to the Romans, and in a saying of our Lord,

"Look up, and lift up your heads, for your redemption draweth nigh."
(Luke 21:28.)

Περιποίησις, which we translate the possession obtained, is not the kingdom of heaven, or a blessed immortality, but the Church itself. This is added for their consolation, that they might not think it hard to cherish their hope till the day of Christ's coming, or be displeased that they have not yet obtained the promised inheritance; for such is the common lot of the whole Church.

To the praise of his glory. The word praise, as in the twelfth verse, Ephesians 1:12 signifies "making known." (116) The glory of God may sometimes be concealed, or imperfectly exhibited. But in the Ephesians God had given proofs of his goodness, that his glory might be celebrated and openly proclaimed. Those persons, therefore, who slighted the calling of the Ephesians, might be charged with envying and slighting the glory of God.

The frequent mention of the glory of God ought not to be regarded as superfluous, for what is infinite cannot be too strongly expressed. This is particularly true in commendations of the Divine mercy, for which every godly person will always feel himself unable to find adequate language. He will be more ready to utter, than other men will be to hear, the expression of praise; for the eloquence both of men and angels, after being strained to the utmost, falls immeasurably below the vastness of this subject. We may likewise observe, that there is not a more effectual method of shutting the mouths of wicked men, than by shewing that our views tend to illustrate, and theirs to obscure, the glory of God.

Verse 15

Wherefore I also. This thanksgiving was not simply an expression of his ardent love to the Ephesians. He congratulated them before God, that the opinion which he had formed respecting them was highly favorable. Observe here, that under faith and love Paul includes generally the whole excellence of Christian character. He uses the expression, faith in the Lord Jesus, (117) because Christ is the aim and object of faith. Love ought to embrace all men, but here the saints are particularly mentioned; because love, when properly regulated, begins with them, and is afterwards extended to all others. If our love must have a view to God, the nearer any man approaches to God, the stronger unquestionably must be his claims to our love.

Verse 16

Making mention of you. To thanksgiving, as his custom is, he adds prayer, in order to excite them to additional progress. It was necessary that the Ephesians should understand that they had entered upon the proper course. But it was equally necessary that they should not turn aside to any new scheme of doctrine, or become indifferent about proceeding farther; for nothing is more dangerous than to be satisfied with that measure of spiritual benefits which has been already obtained. Whatever, then, may be the height of our attainments, let them be always accompanied by the desire of something higher.

Verse 17

That the God of our Lord Jesus Christ. But what does Paul wish for the Ephesians? The spirit of wisdom, and the eyes of their understanding being enlightened. And did they not possess these? Yes; but at the same time they needed increase, that, being endowed with a larger measure of the Spirit, and being more and more enlightened, they might more clearly and fully hold their present views. The knowledge of the godly is never so pure, but that some dimness or obscurity hangs over their spiritual vision. But let us examine the words in detail.

The God of our Lord Jesus Christ. The Son of God became man in such a manner, that God was his God as well as ours.

"I ascend," says he, "to my Father, and your Father; and to my God, and your God." (John 20:17)

And the reason why he is our God, is, that he is the God of Christ, whose members we are. Let us remember, however, that this relates to his human nature; so that his subjection takes nothing away from his eternal godhead.

The Father of glory. This title springs from the former; for God's glory, as a Father, consists in subjecting his Son to our condition, that, through him, he might be our God. The Father of glory is a well-known Hebrew idiom for The glorious Father. There is a mode of pointing and reading this passage, which I do not disapprove, and which connects the two clauses in this manner: That God, the glorious Father of our Lord Jesus Christ, may give to you.

The Spirit of wisdom and revelation is here put, by a figure of speech, (metonymy,) for the grace which the Lord bestows upon us by his own Spirit. But let it be observed, that the gifts of the Spirit are not the gifts of nature. Till the Lord opens them, the eyes of our heart are blind. Till the Spirit has become our instructor, all that we know is folly and ignorance. Till the Spirit of God has made it known to us by a secret revelation, the knowledge of our Divine calling exceeds the capacity of our own minds.

In the knowledge of him. This might also be read, In the knowledge of himself. Both renderings agree well with the context, for he that knows the Son knows also the Father; but I prefer the former as more natively suggested by the Greek pronoun , ἐν

ἐπιγνώσει αὐτοῦ

Verse 18

The eyes of your understanding being enlightened. The eyes of your heart is the rendering of the Vulgate, which is supported by some Greek manuscripts. The difference is immaterial, for the Hebrews frequently employ it to denote the rational powers of the soul, though more strictly, being the seat of the affections, it means the will or desire; but I have preferred the ordinary translation.

And what the riches. A comparison, suggested by its excellence, reminds us how unfit we are to receive this elevated knowledge; for the power of God is no small matter. This great power, he tells us, had been exerted, and in a very extraordinary manner, towards the Ephesians, who were thus laid under constant obligations to follow his calling. By thus extolling the grace of God toward themselves, he intended to check every tendency to despise or dislike the duties of the Christian life. But the splendid encomiums which he pronounces on faith convey to us also this instruction, that it is so admirable a work and gift of God, that no language can do justice to its excellence. Paul is not in the habit of throwing out hyperboles without discrimination; but when he comes to treat of a matter which lies so far beyond this world as faith does, he raises our minds to the admiration of heavenly power.

Verse 19

According to the working. Some consider this clause as referring solely to the word believe, which comes immediately before it; but I rather view it as an additional statement, tending to heighten the greatness of the power, as a demonstration, or, if you prefer it, an instance and evidence of the efficacy of the power. The repetition of the word power, (δυνάμεως) has the appearance of being superfluous; but in the former case it is restricted to one class, — in the next, it has a general application. Paul, we find, never thinks that he can say enough in his descriptions of the Christian calling. And certainly the power of God is wonderfully displayed, when we are brought from death to life, and when, from being the children of hell, we become the children of God and heirs of eternal life.

Foolish men imagine that this language is absurdly hyperbolical; but godly persons, who are engaged in daily struggles with inward corruption, have no difficulty in perceiving that not a word is here used beyond what is perfectly just. As the importance of the subject cannot be too strongly expressed, so our unbelief and ingratitude led Paul to employ this glowing language. We never form adequate conceptions of the treasure revealed to us in the gospel; or, if we do, we cannot persuade ourselves that it is possible for us to do so, because we perceive nothing in us that corresponds to it, but everything the reverse. Paul's object, therefore, was not only to impress the Ephesians with a deep sense of the value of Divine grace, but also to give them exalted views of the glory of Christ's kingdom. That they might not be cast down by a view of their own unworthiness, he exhorts them to consider the power of God; as if he had said, that their regeneration was no ordinary work of God, but was an astonishing exhibition of his power.

According to the efficacy of the power of his strength. There are three words here, on which we may make a passing remark. We may view strength as the root, — power as the tree, — and efficacy as the fruit, or the stretching out of the Divine arm which terminates in action.

Verse 20

Which he wrought in Christ. The Greek verb is ἐνέργησεν, from which ἐνέργεια is derived. It might run thus, According to the efficacy which he effected. But the translation which I have given conveys the same meaning, and is less harsh.

With the greatest propriety does he enjoin us to contemplate this power in Christ; for in us it is hitherto concealed. "My strength," says he, "is made perfect in weakness." (2 Corinthians 12:9.) In what do we excel the children of the world but in this, that our condition appears to be somewhat worse than theirs? Though sin does not reign, it continues to dwell in us, and death is still strong. Our blessedness, which lies in hope, is not perceived by the world. The power of the Spirit is a thing unknown to flesh and blood. A thousand distresses, to which we are daily liable, render us more despised than other men.

Christ alone, therefore, is the mirror in which we can contemplate that which the weakness of the cross hinders from being clearly seen in ourselves. When our minds rise to a confident anticipation of righteousness, salvation, and glory, let us learn to turn them to Christ. We still lie under the power of death; but he, raised from the dead by heavenly power, has the dominion of life. We labor under the bondage of sin, and, surrounded by endless vexations, are engaged in a hard warfare, (1 Timothy 1:18;) but he, sitting at the right hand of the Father, exercises the highest government in heaven and earth, and triumphs gloriously over the enemies whom he has subdued and vanquished. We lie here mean and despised; but to him has been "given a name" (Philippians 2:9,) which angels and men regard with reverence, and devils and wicked men with dread. We are pressed down here by the scantiness of all our comforts: but he has been appointed by the Father to be the sole dispenser of all blessings. For these reasons, we shall find our advantage in directing our views to Christ, that in him, as in a mirror, we may see the glorious treasures of Divine grace, and the unmeasurable greatness of that power, which has not yet been manifested in ourselves.

And set him at his own right hand. This passage shews plainly, if any one does, what is meant by the right hand of God. It does not mean any particular place, but the power which the Father has bestowed on Christ, that he may administer in his name the government of heaven and earth. It is idle, therefore, to inquire why Stephen saw him standing, (Acts 7:55,) while Paul describes him as sitting at God's right hand. The expression does not refer to any bodily posture, but denotes the highest royal power with which Christ has been invested. This is intimated by what immediately follows, far above all principality and power: for the whole of this description is added for the purpose of explaining what is meant bythe right hand.

God the Father is said to have raised Christ to "his right hand," because he has made him to share in his government, because by him he exerts all his power; the metaphor being borrowed from earthly princes, who confer the honor of sitting along with themselves on those whom they have clothed with the highest authority. As the right hand of God fills heaven and earth, it follows that the kingdom and power of Christ are equally extensive. It is in vain, therefore, to attempt to prove that, because Christ sitteth at the right hand of God, he dwells in heaven alone. His human nature, it is true, resides in heaven, and not in earth; but that argument is foreign to the purpose. The expression which follows, in heavenly places, does not at all imply that the right hand of God is confined to heaven, but directs us to contemplate the heavenly glory amidst which our Lord Jesus dwells, the blessed immortality which he enjoys, and the dominion over angels to which he has been exalted.

Verse 21

Far above all principality, and power, and might, and dominion. All these names, there can be no doubt, are applied to angels, who are so denominated, because, by means of them, God exercises his power, and might, and dominion. He permits them to share, as far as is competent to creatures, what belongs to himself, and even gives to them his own name; for we find that they are called אלהים, (elohim,) gods. From the diversity of names we conclude that there are various orders of angels; but to attempt to settle these with exactness, to fix their number, or determine their ranks, would not merely discover foolish curiosity, but would be rash, wicked, and dangerous.

But why did he not simply call them Angels? I answer, it was to convey exalted views of the glory of Christ that Paul employed those lofty titles. As if he had said, "There is nothing so elevated or excellent, by whatever name it may be named, that is not subject to the majesty of Christ." There was an ancient superstition, prevalent both among Jews and Gentiles, falsely attributing to angels many things, in order to draw away their minds from God himself, and from the true Mediator. Paul constantly labors to prevent this imaginary lustre of angels from dazzling the eyes of men, or obscuring the brightness of Christ; and yet his utmost exertions could not prevent "the wiles of the devil"(Ephesians 6:11) from succeeding in this matter. Thus we see how the world, through a superstitious dread of angels, departed from Christ. It was indeed the unavoidable consequence of the false opinions entertained respecting angels, that the pure knowledge of Christ disappeared.

Above every name that is named. Name is here taken for largeness, or excellence; and to be named means to enjoy celebrity and praise. The age that is to come is expressly mentioned, to point out that the exalted rank of Christ is not temporal, but eternal; and that it is not limited to this world, but shines illustriously in the kingdom of God. For this reason, too, Isaiah calls him, (Isaiah 9:6,) The Father of the future age. In short, the glories of men and angels are made to hold an inferior place, that the glory of Christ, unequalled and unapproached, may shine above them all.

Verse 22

And gave him to be the head. He was made the head of the Church, on the condition that he should have the administration of all things. The apostle shews that it was not a mere honorary title, but was accompanied by the entire command and government of the universe. The metaphor of a head denotes the highest authority. I am unwilling to dispute about a name, but we are driven to it by the base conduct of those who flatter the Romish idol. Since Christ alone is called "the head," all others, whether angels or men, must rank as members; so that he who holds the highest place among his fellows is still one of the members of the same body. And yet they are not ashamed to make an open avowal that the Church will be ἀκέφαλον, without a head, if it has not another head on earth besides Christ. So small is the respect which they pay to Christ, that, if he obtain undivided that honor which his Father has bestowed upon him, the Church is supposed to be disfigured. This is the basest sacrilege. But let us listen to the Apostle, who declares that the Church is His body, and, consequently, that those who refuse to submit to Him are unworthy of its communion; for on Him alone the unity of the Church depends.

Verse 23

The fullness of him that filleth all in all. This is the highest honor of the Church, that, until He is united to us, the Son of God reckons himself in some measure imperfect. What consolation is it for us to learn, that, not until we are along with him, does he possess all his parts, or wish to be regarded as complete! Hence, in the First Epistle to the Corinthians, [1 Corinthians 12:12] when the apostle discusses largely the metaphor of a human body, he includes under the single name of Christ the whole Church.

That filleth all in all. This is added to guard against the supposition that any real defect would exist in Christ, if he were separated from us. His wish to be filled, and, in some respects, made perfect in us, arises from no want or necessity; for all that is good in ourselves, or in any of the creatures, is the gift of his hand; and his goodness appears the more remarkably in raising us out of nothing, that he, in like manner, may dwell and live in us. There is no impropriety in limiting the word all to its application to this passage; for, though all things are regulated by the will and power of Christ, yet the subject of which Paul particularly speaks is the spiritual government of the Church. There is nothing, indeed, to hinder us from viewing it as referring to the universal government of the world; but to limit it to the case in hand is the more probable interpretation.

CALVIN EPHESIANS 2

Verse 1

And you who were dead. This is an ἐπεξεργασία of the former statements, that is, an exposition accompanied by an illustration. (118) To bring home more effectually to the Ephesians the general doctrine of Divine grace, he reminds them of their former condition. This application consists of two parts. "Ye were formerly lost; but now God, by his grace, has rescued you from destruction." And here we must observe, that, in laboring to give an impressive view of both of these parts, the apostle makes a break in the style by (ὑπερβατὸν) a transposition. There is some perplexity in the language; but, if we attend carefully to what the apostle says about those two parts, the meaning is clear. As to the first, he says that they were dead; and states, at the same time, the cause of the death — trespasses and sins. (119) He does not mean simply that they were in danger of death; but he declares that it was a real and present death under which they labored. As spiritual death is nothing else than the alienation of the soul from God, we are all born as dead men, and we live as dead men, until we are made partakers of the life of Christ, — agreeably to the words of our Lord,

"The hour is coming, and now is, when the dead shall hear the voice of the Son of God, and they that hear shall live." (John 5:25)

The Papists, who are eager to seize every opportunity of undervaluing the grace of God, say, that while we are out of Christ, we are half dead. But we are not at liberty to set aside the declarations of our Lord and of the Apostle Paul, that, while we remain in Adam, we are entirely devoid of life; and that regeneration is a new life of the soul, by which it rises from the dead. Some kind of life, I acknowledge, does remain in us, while we are still at a distance from Christ; for unbelief does not altogether destroy the outward senses, or the will, or the other faculties of the soul. But what has this to do with the kingdom of God? What has it to do with a happy life, so long as every sentiment of the mind, and every act of the will, is death? Let this, then, be held as a fixed principle, that the union of our soul with God is the true and only life; and that out of Christ we are altogether dead, because sin, the cause of death, reigns in us.

Verse 2

In which for some time ye walked. From the effects or fruits, he draws a proof that sin formerly reigned in them; for, until sin displays itself in outward acts, men are not sufficiently aware of its power. When he adds, according to the course of this world, (120) he intimates that the death which he had mentioned rages in the nature of

26

man, and is a universal disease. He does not mean that course of the world which God has ordained, nor the elements, such as the heaven, and earth, and air, — but the depravity with which we are all infected; so that sin is not peculiar to a few, but pervades the whole world.

According to the prince of the power of the air. He now proceeds farther, and explains the cause of our corruption to be the dominion which the devil exercises over us. A more severe condemnation of mankind could not have been pronounced. What does he leave to us, when he declares us to be the slaves of Satan, and subject to his will, so long as we live out of the kingdom of Christ? Our condition, therefore, though many treat it with ridicule, or, at least, with little disapprobation, may well excite our horror. Where is now the free-will, the guidance of reason, the moral virtue, about which Papists babble to much? What will they find that is pure or holy under the tyranny of the devil? On this subject, indeed, they are extremely cautious, and denounce this doctrine of Paul as a grievous heresy. I maintain, on the contrary, that there is no obscurity in the apostle's language; and that all men who live according to the world, that is, according to the inclinations of their flesh, are here declared to fight under the reign of Satan.

In accordance with the practice of the inspired writers, the Devil is mentioned in the singular number. As the children of God have one head, so have the wicked; for each of the classes forms a distinct body. By assigning to him the dominion over all wicked beings, ungodliness is represented as an unbroken mass. As to his attributing to the devil power over the air, that will be considered when we come to the sixth chapter. At present, we shall merely advert to the strange absurdity of the Manicheans, in endeavoring to prove from this passage the existence of two principles, as if Satan could do anything without the Divine permission. Paul does not allow him the highest authority, which belongs to the will of God alone, but merely a tyranny which God permits him to exercise. What is Satan but God's executioner to punish man's ingratitude? This is implied in Paul's language, when he represents the success of Satan as confined to unbelievers; for the children of God are thus exempted from his power. If this be true, it follows that Satan does nothing but under the control of a superior: and that he is not (αὐτοκράτωρ) an unlimited monarch.

We may now draw from it also this inference, that ungodly men have no excuse in being driven by Satan to commit all sorts of crimes. Whence comes it that they are subject to his tyranny, but because they are rebels against God? If none are the slaves of Satan, but those who have renounced the service, and refuse to yield to the authority, of God, let them blame themselves, for having so cruel a master.

By the children of disobedience, according to a Hebrew idiom, are meant obstinate persons. Unbelief is always accompanied by disobedience; so that it is the source — the mother of all stubbornness.

Verse 3

Among whom also we all had our conversation. Lest it should be supposed that what he had now said was a slanderous reproach against the former character of the Ephesians, or that Jewish pride had led him to treat the Gentiles as an inferior race, he associates himself and his countrymen along with them in the general accusation. This is not done in hypocrisy, but in a sincere ascription of glory to God. It may excite wonder, indeed, that he should speak of himself as having walked "in the lusts of the flesh," while, on other occasions, he boasts that his life had been throughout irreproachable.

"Touching the righteousness which is in the law, blameless." (Philippians 3:6.)

And again,

"Ye are witnesses, and God also, how holily, and justly, and unblamably, we behaved ourselves among you that believe."
(1 Thessalonians 2:10)

I reply, the statement applies to all who have not been regenerated by the Spirit of Christ. However praiseworthy, in appearance, the life of some may be, because their lusts do not break out in the sight of men, there is nothing pure or holy which does not proceed from the fountain of all purity.

Fulfilling the desires of the flesh and of the mind. To fulfill these desires, is to live according to the guidance of our natural disposition and of our mind. The flesh means here the disposition, or, what is called, the inclination of the nature; and the next expression (τῶν διανοιῶν) means what proceeds from the mind. Now, the mind includes reason, such as it exists in men by nature; so that lusts do not refer exclusively to the lower appetites, or what is called the sensual part of man, but extend to the whole.

And were by nature (121) children of wrath. All men without exception, whether Jews or Gentiles, (Galatians 2:15,) are here pronounced to be guilty, until they are redeemed by Christ; so that out of Christ there is no righteousness, no salvation, and, in short, no excellence. Children of wrath are those who are lost, and who deserve eternal death. Wrath means the judgment of God; so that the children of wrath are those who are condemned before God. Such, the apostle tells us, had been the Jews, — such had been all the excellent men that were now in the Church; and they were so by nature, that is, from their very commencement, and from their mother's womb.

This is a remarkable passage, in opposition to the views of the Pelagians, and of all who deny original sin. What dwells naturally in all is certainly original; but Paul declares that we are all naturally liable to condemnation; therefore sin dwells naturally in us, for God does not condemn the innocent. Pelagians were wont to object, that sin spread from Adam to the whole human race, not by descent, but by imitation. But Paul affirms that we are born with sin, as serpents bring their venom from the womb. Others who think that it is not in reality sin, are not less at variance with Paul's language; for where condemnation is, there must unquestionably be sin. It is not with blameless men, but with sin, that God is offended. Nor is it wonderful that the depravity which we inherit from our parents is reckoned as sin before God; for the seeds of sin, before they have been openly displayed, are perceived and condemned.

But one question here arises. Why does Paul represent the Jews, equally with others, as subject to wrath and curse, while they were the blessed seed? I answer, they have a common nature. Jews differ from Gentiles in nothing but this, that, through the grace of the promise, God delivers them from destruction; but that is a remedy which came after the disease. Another question is, since God is the Author of nature, how comes it that no blame attaches to God, if we are lost by nature? I answer, there is a twofold nature: the one was produced by God, and the other is the corruption of it. This condemnation therefore which Paul mentions does not proceed from God, but from a depraved nature: for we are not born such as Adam was at first created, we are not

"wholly a right seed, but are turned into the degenerate"
(Jeremiah 2:21)

offspring of a degenerate and sinful man.

Verse 4

But God, who is rich in mercy. (122) Now follows the second member of the sentence, the substance of which is, that God had delivered the Ephesians from the destruction to which they were formerly liable; but the words which he employs are different. God, who is rich in mercy, hath quickened you together with Christ. The meaning is, that, there is no other life than that which is breathed into us by Christ: so that we begin to live only when we are ingrafted into him, and enjoy the same life with himself. This enables us to see what the apostle formerly meant by death, for that death and this resurrection are brought into contrast. To be made partakers of the life of the Son of God, — to be quickened by one Spirit, is an inestimable privilege.

On this ground he praises the mercy of God, meaning by its riches, that it had been poured out in a singularly large and abundant manner. The whole of our salvation is here ascribed to the mercy of God. But he presently adds, for his great love wherewith he loved us. (123) This is a still more express declaration, that all was owing to undeserved goodness; for he declares that God was moved by this single consideration. "Herein," says John, "is love, not that we loved God, but that he loved us. — We love him because he first loved us." (1 John 4:10.)

Verse 5

Even when we were dead in sin. These words have the same emphasis as similar expressions in another Epistle.

"For when we were yet without strength, in due time Christ died, for the ungodly. — But God commendeth his love toward us, in that, while we were yet sinners, Christ died for us."
(Romans 5:6.)

Whether the words, by grace ye are saved, have been inserted by another hand, I know not; but, as they are perfectly agreeable to the context, I am quite willing to receive them as written by Paul. They show us that he always feels as if he had not sufficiently proclaimed the riches of Divine grace, and accordingly expresses, by a variety of terms, the same truth, that everything connected with our salvation ought to be ascribed to God as its author. And certainly he who duly weighs the ingratitude of men will not complain that this parenthesis is superfluous.

Verse 6

And hath raised us up together. The resurrection and sitting in heaven, which are here mentioned, are not yet seen by mortal eyes. Yet, as if those blessings were presently in our possession, he states that we have received them; and illustrates the change which has taken place in our condition, when we were led from Adam to Christ. It is as if we had been brought from the deepest hell to heaven itself. And certainly, although, as respects ourselves, our salvation is still the object of hope, yet in Christ we already possess a blessed immortality and glory; and therefore, he adds, in Christ Jesus. Hitherto it does not appear in the members, but only in the head; yet, in consequence of the secret union, it belongs truly to the members. Some render it, through Christ; but, for the reason which has been mentioned, it is better to retain the usual rendering, in Christ. We are thus furnished with the richest consolation. Of everything which we now want, we have a sure pledge and foretaste in the person of Christ.

Verse 7

That in the ages to come. The final and true cause — the glory of God — is again mentioned, that the Ephesians, by making it the subject of earnest study, might be more fully assured of their salvation. He likewise adds, that it was the design of God to hallow, in all ages, the remembrance of so great goodness. This exhibits still more strongly the hateful character of those by whom the free calling of the Gentiles was attacked; for they were endeavoring instantly to crush that scheme which was destined to be remembered through all ages. But we, too, are instructed by it, that the mercy of God, who was pleased to admit our fathers into the number of his own people, deserves to be held in everlasting remembrance. The calling of the Gentiles is an astonishing work of divine goodness, which ought to be handed down by parents to children, and to their children's children, that it may never be forgotten or unacknowledged by the sons of men.

The riches of his grace in his kindness. The love of God to us in Christ is here proved, or again declared, to have had its origin in mercy. That he might shew, says he, the exceeding riches of his grace. How? In his kindness towards us, as the tree is known by its fruit. Not only, therefore, does he declare, that the love of God was free, but likewise that God displayed in it the riches, — the extraordinary pre-eminent riches of his grace. It deserves notice, also, that the name ofChrist is repeated; for no grace, no love, must be expected by us from God, except through his mediation.

Verse 8

For by grace are ye saved. This is an inference from the former statements. Having treated of election and of effectual calling, he arrives at this general conclusion, that they had obtained salvation by faith alone. First, he asserts, that the salvation of the Ephesians was entirely the work, the gracious work of God. But then they had obtained this grace by faith. On one side, we must look at God; and, on the other, at man. God declares, that he owes us nothing; so that salvation is not a reward or recompense, but unmixed grace. The next question is, in what way do men receive that salvation which is offered to them by the hand of God? The answer is, by faith; and hence he concludes that nothing connected with it is our own. If, on the part of God, it is grace alone, and if we bring nothing but faith, which strips us of all commendation, it follows that salvation does not come from us.

Ought we not then to be silent about free-will, and good intentions, and fancied preparations, and merits, and satisfactions? There is none of these which does not claim a share of praise in the salvation of men; so that the praise of grace would not, as Paul shews, remain undiminished. When, on the part of man, the act of receiving salvation is made to consist in faith alone, all other means, on which men are accustomed to rely, are discarded. Faith, then, brings a man empty to God, that he may be filled with the blessings of Christ. And so he adds, not of yourselves; that claiming nothing for themselves, they may acknowledge God alone as the author of their salvation.

Verse 9

Not of works. Instead of what he had said, that their salvation is of grace, he now affirms, that "it is the gift of God." (124) Instead of what he had said, " Not of yourselves," he now says, " Not of works." Hence we see, that the apostle leaves nothing to men in procuring salvation. In these three phrases, — not of yourselves, — it is the gift of God, — not of works, — he embraces the substance of his long argument in the Epistles to the Romans and to the Galatians, that righteousness comes to us from the mercy of God alone, — is offered to us in Christ by the gospel, — and is received by faith alone, without the merit of works.

This passage affords an easy refutation of the idle cavil by which Papists attempt to evade the argument, that we are justified without works. Paul, they tell us, is speaking about ceremonies. But the present question is not confined to one class of works. Nothing can be more clear than this. The whole righteousness of man, which consists in works, — nay, the whole man, and everything that he can call his own, is set aside. We must attend to the contrast between God and man, — between grace and works. Why should God be contrasted with man, if the controversy related to nothing more than ceremonies?

Papists themselves are compelled to own that Paul ascribes to the grace of God the whole glory of our salvation, but endeavor to do away with this admission by another contrivance. This mode of expression, they tell us, is employed, because God bestows the first grace. It is really foolish to imagine that they can succeed in this way, since Paul excludes man and his utmost ability, — not only from the commencement, but throughout, — from the whole work of obtaining salvation.

But it is still more absurd to overlook the apostle's inference,lest any man should boast. Some room must always remain for man's boasting, so long as, independently of grace, merits are of any avail. Paul's doctrine is overthrown, unless the whole praise is rendered to God alone and to his mercy. And here we must advert to a very common error in the interpretation of this passage. Many persons restrict the word gift to faith alone. But Paul is only repeating in other words the former sentiment. His meaning is, not that faith is the gift of God, but that salvation is given to us by God, or, that we obtain it by the gift of God.

Verse 10

For we are his work. By setting aside the contrary supposition, he proves his statement, that by grace we are saved, — that we have no remaining works by which we can merit salvation; for all the good works which we possess are the fruit of regeneration. Hence it follows, that works themselves are a part of grace.

When he says, that "we are the work of God," this does not refer to ordinary creation, by which we are made men. We are declared to be new creatures, because, not by our own power, but by the Spirit of Christ, we have been formed to righteousness. This applies to none but believers. As the descendants of Adam, they were wicked and depraved; but by the grace of Christ, they are spiritually renewed, and become new men. Everything in us, therefore, that is good, is the supernatural gift of God. The context explains his meaning. We are his work, because we have been created, — not in Adam, but in Christ Jesus, — not to every kind of life, but to good works.

What remains now for free-will, if all the good works which proceed from us are acknowledged to have been the gifts of the Spirit of God? Let godly readers weigh carefully the apostle's words. He does not say that we are assisted by God. He does not say that the will is prepared, and is then left to run by its own strength. He does not say that the power of choosing aright is bestowed upon us, and that we are afterwards left to make our own choice. Such is the idle talk in which those persons who do their utmost to undervalue the grace of God are accustomed to indulge. But the apostle affirms that we are God's work, and that everything good in us is his creation; by which he means that the whole man is formed by his hand to be good. It is not the mere power of choosing aright, or some indescribable kind of preparation, or even assistance, but the right will itself, which is his workmanship; otherwise Paul's argument would have no force. He means to prove that man does not in any way procure salvation for himself, but obtains it as a free gift from God. The proof is, that man is nothing but by divine grace. Whoever, then, makes the very smallest claim for man, apart from the grace of God, allows him, to that extent, ability to procure salvation.

Created to good works. They err widely from Paul's intention, who torture this passage for the purpose of injuring the righteousness of faith. Ashamed to affirm in plain terms, and aware that they could gain nothing by affirming, that we are not justified by faith, they shelter themselves under this kind of subterfuge. "We are justified by faith, because faith, by which we receive the grace of God, is the commencement of righteousness; but we are made righteous by regeneration, because, being renewed by the Spirit of God, we walk in good works." In this manner they make faith the door by which we enter into righteousness, but imagine that we obtain it by our works, or, at least, they define righteousness to be that uprightness by which a man is formed anew to a holy life. I care not how old this error may be; but they err egregiously who endeavor to support it by this passage.

We must look to Paul's design. He intends to shew that we have brought nothing to God, by which he might be laid under obligations to us; and he shews that even the good works which we perform have come from God. Hence it follows, that we are nothing, except through the pure exercise of his kindness. Those men, on the other hand, infer that the half of our justification arises from works. But what has this to do with Paul's intention, or with the subject which he handles? It is one thing to inquire in what righteousness consists, and another thing to follow up the doctrine, that it is not from ourselves, by this argument, that we have no right to claim good works as our own, but have been formed by the Spirit of God, through the grace of Christ, to all that is good. When Paul lays down the cause of justification, he dwells chiefly on this point, that our consciences will never enjoy peace till they rely on the propitiation for sins. Nothing of this sort is even alluded to in the present instance. His whole object is to prove, that,

"by the grace of God, we are all that we are."
(1 Corinthians 15:10)

Which God hath prepared Beware of applying this, as the Pelagians do, to the instruction of the law; as if Paul's meaning were, that God commands what is just, and lays down a proper rule of life. Instead of this, he follows up the doctrine which he had begun to illustrate, that salvation does not proceed from ourselves. He says, that, before we were born, the good works were prepared by God; meaning, that in our own strength we are not able to lead a holy life, but only so far as we are formed and adapted by the hand of God. Now, if the grace of God came before our performances, all ground of boasting has been taken away. Let us carefully observe the word prepared. On the simple ground of the order of events, Paul rests the proof that, with respect to good works, God owes us nothing. How so? Because they were drawn out of his treasures, in which they had long before been laid up; for whom he called, them he justifies and regenerates.

Verse 11

Wherefore remember. The apostle never once loses sight of his subject, marks it out clearly, and pursues it with increasing earnestness. He again exhorts the Ephesians to remember what their character had been before they were called. This consideration was fitted to convince them that they had no reason to be proud. He afterwards points out the method of reconciliation, that they might rest with perfect satisfaction on Christ alone, and not imagine that other aids were necessary. The first clause may be thus summed up: "Remember that, when ye were uncircumcised, ye were aliens from Christ, from the hope of salvation, and from the Church and kingdom of God; so that ye had no friendly intercourse with God." The second may run thus: "But now ingrafted into Christ, ye are at the same time reconciled to God." What is implied in both parts of the description, and what effect the remembrance of it was fitted to produce on their minds, has been already considered.

Gentiles in the flesh. He first mentions that they had wanted the marks of God's people. Circumcision was a token by which the people of God were marked out and distinguished from other men: Uncircumcision was the mark of a profane person. Since, therefore, God usually connects his grace with the sacraments, their want of the sacraments is taken as an evidence that neither were they partakers of his grace. The argument, indeed, does not hold universally, though it does hold as to God's ordinary dispensations. Hence we find the following language:

"And the Lord God said, Behold, the man is become as one of us, to know good and evil: and now, lest he put forth his hand, and take also of the tree of life, and eat, and live for ever: therefore the Lord God sent him forth from the garden of Eden, to till the ground from whence he was taken. So he drove out the man."
(Genesis 3:22)

Though he had devoured the whole tree, he would not, by merely eating it, have recovered the possession of life; but, by taking away the sign, the Lord took from him also life itself. Uncircumcision is thus held out to the Ephesians as a mark of pollution. By taking from the Ephesians the token of sanctification, he deprives them also of the thing signified.

Some are of opinion, that all these observations are intended to throw contempt on outward circumcision; but this is a mistake. At the same time, I acknowledge, that the qualifying clause, the Circumcision in the flesh made by hands, points out a twofold circumcision. The Jews were thus taught that they should no longer indulge in foolish boasting about the literal circumcision. The Ephesians, on the other hand, were instructed to abstain from all scruples on their own account, since the most important privilege—nay, the whole truth expressed by the outward sign—was in their possession. He calls it, Uncircumcision in the flesh, because they bore the mark of their pollution; but, at the same time, he suggests that their uncircumcision was no hinderance to their being spiritually circumcised by Christ.

The words may likewise be read in one clause, Circumcision in the flesh made by hands, or in two clauses: Circumcision in the flesh, meaning that it was carnal;made by hands, meaning that it was done by the hand of man. This kind of circumcision is contrasted with that of the Spirit, or of the heart, (Romans 2:29,) which is also called the circumcision of Christ. (Colossians 2:11)

By that which is called. Circumcision may be viewed here either as a collective noun for the Jews themselves, or literally for the thing itself; and then the meaning would be, that the Gentiles were called Uncircumcision, because they wanted the sacred symbol, that is, by way of distinction. This latter sense is countenanced by the qualifying phrase; but the substance of the argument is little affected.

Verse 12

That at that time ye were without Christ. He now declares that the Ephesians had been excluded, not only from the outward badge, but from everything necessary to the salvation and happiness of men. As Christ is the foundation of hope and of all the promises, he mentions, first of all, that they were without Christ. But for him that is without Christ, there remains nothing but destruction. On Him the commonwealth of Israel was founded; and in whom, but in Himself, could the people of God be collected into one holy society?

A similar observation might be made as to the tables of the promise On one great promise made to Abraham all the others hang, and without it they lose all their value:

"In thy seed shall all the nations of the earth be blessed."
(Genesis 22:18.)

Hence our apostle says elsewhere,

"All the promises of God in him are yea, and in him Amen."
(2 Corinthians 1:20.)

Take away the covenant of salvation, and there remains no hope. I have translated τῶν διαθηκῶν by the tables, or, in ordinary legal phrase, the instruments. By solemn ritual did God sanction His covenant with Abraham and his posterity, that he would be their God for ever and ever. (Genesis 15:9.) Tables of this covenant were ratified by the hand of Moses, and intrusted, as a peculiar treasure, to the people of Israel, to whom, and not to the Gentiles, "pertain the covenants." (Romans 9:4.)

And without God in the world. But at no period were the Ephesians, or any other Gentiles, destitute of all religion. Why, then, are they styled (ἄθεοι) Atheists? for (ἄθεος) an Atheist, strictly speaking, is one who does not believe, and who absolutely ridicules, the being of a God. That appellation, certainly, is not usually given to superstitious persons, but to those who have no feeling of religion, and who desire to see it utterly destroyed. I answer, Paul was right in giving them this name, for he treated all the notions entertained respecting false gods as nothing; and with the utmost propriety do godly persons regard all idols as "nothing in the world." (1 Corinthians 8:4.) Those who do not worship the true God, whatever may be the variety of their worship, or the multitude of laborious ceremonies which they perform, are without God: they adore what they know not. (Acts 17:23.) Let it be carefully observed, that the Ephesians are not charged with (ἀθεϊσμὸς) Atheism, in the same degree as Diagoras, and others of the same stamp, who were subjected to that reproach. Persons who imagined themselves to be very religious are charged with that crime; for an idol is a forgery, an imposition, not a Divinity.

From what has been said, the conclusion will be easily drawn, that out of Christ there are none but idols. Those who were formerly declared to be without Christ, are now declared to be without God; (125) as John says,

"Whosoever hath not the Son, hath not the Father,"
(1 John 2:23;)

and again,

"Whosoever transgresseth, and abideth not in the doctrine of Christ, hath not God."
(2 John 1:9.)

Let us know, therefore, that all who do not keep this way wander from the true God. We shall next be asked, Did God never reveal himself to any of the Gentiles? I answer, no manifestation of God without Christ was ever made among the Gentiles, any more than among the Jews. It is not to one age only, or to one nation, that the saying of our Lord applies,

"I am the way;" for he adds, "no man cometh
unto the Father but by me." (John 14:6.)

Verse 13

But now in Christ Jesus. We must either supply the verb, now that ye have been received in Christ Jesus, or connect the word now with the conclusion of the verse, now through the blood of Christ, — which will be a still clearer exposition. In either case, the meaning is, that the Ephesians, who were far off from God and from salvation, had been reconciled to God through Christ, and made nigh by his blood; for the blood of Christ has taken away the enmity which existed between them and God, and from being enemies hath made them sons.

Verse 14

For he is our peace. He now includes Jews in the privilege of reconciliation, and shows that, through one Messiah, all are united to God. This consideration was fitted to repress the false confidence of the Jews, who, despising the grace of Christ, boasted that they were the holy people, and chosen inheritance, of God. If Christ is our peace, all who are out of him must be at variance with God. What a beautiful title is this which Christ possesses, — the peace between God and men! Let no one who dwells in Christ entertain a doubt that he is reconciled to God.

Who hath made both one. This distinction was necessary. (126) All intercourse with the Gentiles was held to be inconsistent with their own superior claims. (127) To subdue this pride, he tells them that they and the Gentiles have been united into one body. Put all these things together, and you will frame the following syllogism: If the Jews wish to enjoy peace with God, they must have Christ as their Mediator. But Christ will not be their peace in any other way than by making them one body with the Gentiles. Therefore, unless the Jews admit the Gentiles to fellowship with them, they have no friendship with God.

And breaking down the middle wall of partition. To understand this passage, two things must be observed. The Jews were separated, for a certain time, from the Gentiles, by the appointment of God; and ceremonial observances were the open and avowed symbols of that separation. Passing by the Gentiles, God had chosen

38

the Jews to be a peculiar people to himself. A wide distinction was thus made, when the one class were "fellow-citizens and of the household" (Ephesians 2:19) of the Church, and the other were foreigners. This is stated in the Song of Moses:

"When the Most High divided to the nations their inheritance, when he separated the sons of Adam, he set the bounds of the people according to the number of the children of Israel: for the Lord's portion is his people, Jacob is the lot of his inheritance." (Deuteronomy 32:8)

Bounds were thus fixed by God to separate one people from the rest; and hence arose the enmity which is here mentioned. A separation is thus made. The Gentiles are set aside. God is pleased to choose and sanctify the Jewish people, by freeing them from the ordinary pollution of mankind. Ceremonial observances were afterwards added, which, like walls, enclosed the inheritance of God, prevented it from being open to all or mixed with other possessions, and thus excluded the Gentiles from the kingdom of God.

But now, the apostle, says, the enmity is removed, and the wall is broken down. By extending the privilege of adoption beyond the limits of Judea, Christ has now made us all to be brethren. And so is fulfilled the prophecy,

"God shall enlarge Japheth,
and he shall dwell in the tents of Shem." (Genesis 9:27)

Verse 15

Having abolished in his flesh the enmity. The meaning of Paul's words is now clear. The middle wall of partition hindered Christ from forming Jews and Gentiles into one body, and therefore the wall has been broken down. The reason why it is broken down is now added — to abolish the enmity, by the flesh of Christ. The Son of God, by assuming a nature common to all, has formed in his own body a perfect unity.

Even the law of commandments contained in ordinances. What had been metaphorically understood by the word wall is now more plainly expressed. The ceremonies, by which the distinction was declared, have been abolished through Christ. What were circumcision, sacrifices, washings, and abstaining from certain kinds of food, but symbols of sanctification, reminding the Jews that their lot was different from that of other nations; just as the white and the red cross distinguish the French of the present day from the inhabitants of Burgundy. Paul declares not only that the Gentiles are equally with the Jews admitted to the fellowship of grace, so that they no longer differ from each other, but that the mark of difference has been taken away; for ceremonies have been abolished. If two contending nations were brought under the dominion of one prince, he would not only desire that they should live in harmony, but would remove the badges and marks of their former enmity. When an obligation is discharged, the handwriting is destroyed, — a metaphor which Paul employs on this very subject in another Epistle. (128) (Colossians 2:14.)

Some interpreters, (129) — though, in my opinion, erroneously, — connect the words, in ordinances, with abolished, making the ordinances to be the act of abolishing the ceremonies. This is Paul's ordinary phrase for describing the ceremonial law, in which the Lord not only enjoined upon the Jews a simple rule of life, but also bound them by various statutes. It is evident, too, that Paul is here treating exclusively of the ceremonial law; for the moral law is not a wall of partition separating us from the Jews, but lays down instructions in which the Jews were not less deeply concerned than ourselves. This passage affords the means of refuting an erroneous view held by some, that circumcision and all the ancient rites, though they are not binding on the Gentiles, are in force at the present day upon the Jews. On this principle there would still be a middle wall of partition between us, which is proved to be false.

That he might make in himself. When the apostle says, in himself, he turns away the Ephesians from viewing the diversity of men, and bids them look for unity nowhere but in Christ. To whatever extent the two might differ in their former condition, in Christ they are become one man. But he emphatically adds, one new man, intimating (what he explains at greater length on another occasion) that

"neither circumcision, nor uncircumcision, availeth anything," (Galatians 6:15,)

but that "a new creature" holds the first and the last place. The principle which cements them is spiritual regeneration. If then we are all renewed by Christ, let the Jews no longer congratulate themselves on their ancient condition, but let them be ready to admit that, both in themselves and in others, Christ is all.

Verse 16

And that he might reconcile both. The reconciliation between ourselves which has now been described is not the only advantage which we derive from Christ. We have been brought back into favor with God. The Jews are thus led to consider that they have not less need of a Mediator than the Gentiles. Without this, neither the Law, nor ceremonies, nor their descent from Abraham, nor all their dazzling prerogatives, would be of any avail. We are all sinners; and forgiveness of sins cannot be obtained but through the grace of Christ. He adds, in one body, to inform the Jews, that to cultivate union with the Gentiles will be well-pleasing in the sight of God.

By the cross. The word cross is added, to point out the propitiatory sacrifice. Sin is the cause of enmity between God and us; and, until it is removed, we shall not be restored to the Divine favor. It has been blotted out by the death of Christ, in which he offered himself to the Father as an expiatory victim. There is another reason, indeed, why the cross is mentioned here, as it is through the cross that all ceremonies have been abolished. Accordingly, he adds, slaying the enmity thereby. These words, which unquestionably relate to the cross, may admit of two senses, — either that Christ, by his death, has turned away from us the Father's anger, or that, having redeemed both Jews and Gentiles, he has brought them back into one flock. The latter appears to be the more probable interpretation, as it agrees with a former clause, abolishing in his flesh the enmity. (Ephesians 2:15.)

Verse 17

And came and preached peace. All that Christ had done towards effecting a reconciliation would have been of no service, if it had not been proclaimed by the gospel; and therefore he adds, that the fruit of this peace has now been offered both to Jews and to Gentiles. Hence it follows, that to save Gentiles as well as Jews was the design of our Savior's coming, as the preaching of the gospel, which is addressed indiscriminately to both, makes abundantly manifest. The same order is followed in the second Epistle to the Corinthians.

"He hath committed to us the word of reconciliation. Now, then, we are ambassadors for Christ. For he hath made him to be sin for us who knew no sin." (2 Corinthians 5:18.)

Salvation through the death of Christ is first announced, and a description is afterwards given of the manner in which Christ communicates to us himself and the benefit of his death. But here Paul dwells chiefly on this circumstance, that Gentiles are united with Jews in the Kingdom of God. Having already represented Christ as a Savior common to both, he now speaks of them as companions in the gospel. The Jews, though they possessed the law, needed the gospel also; and God had bestowed upon the Gentiles equal grace. Those therefore whom

"God hath joined together, let no man put asunder."
(Matthew 19:6.)

No reference to distance of place is conveyed by the words afar off and nigh. The Jews, in respect of the covenant, were nigh to God. The Gentiles, so long as they had no promise of salvation, were afar off — were banished from the kingdom of God.

And preached peace; not indeed by his own lips, but by the apostles. It was necessary that Christ should rise from the dead, before the Gentiles were called to the fellowship of grace. Hence that saying of our Lord,

"I am not sent but to the lost sheep of the house of Israel." (Matthew 15:24.)

The apostles were forbidden, while he was still in the world, to carry their first embassy to the Gentiles.

"Go not into the way of the Gentiles, and into any city of the Samaritans, enter ye not. But go rather to the lost sheep of the house of Israel." (Matthew 10:5,)

His apostles were afterwards employed as trumpets for proclaiming the gospel to the Gentiles. What they did, not only in his name, and by his command, but as it were in his own person, is justly ascribed to none other than himself. We too speak as if Christ himself exhorted you by us. (2 Corinthians 5:20) The faith of the gospel would be weak indeed, were we to look no higher than to men. Its whole authority is derived from viewing men as God's instruments, and hearing Christ speak to us by their mouth. Observe here, the gospel is the message of peace, by which God declares himself to be reconciled to us, and makes known his paternal love. Take away the gospel, and war and enmity continue to subsist between God and men; and, on the other hand, the native tendency of the gospel is, to give peace and calmness to the conscience, which would otherwise be tormented by distressing alarm.

Verse 18

For through him we both have access. This is an argument from the fact, that we are permitted to draw near to God. But it may be viewed also as an announcement of peace; for wicked men, lulled into a profound sleep, sometimes deceive themselves by false notions of peace, but are never at rest, except when they have learned to forget the Divine judgment, and to keep themselves at the greatest possible distance from God. It was necessary, therefore, to explain the true nature of evangelical peace, which is widely different from a stupefied conscience, from false confidence, from proud boasting, from ignorance of our own wretchedness. It is a settled composure, which leads us not to dread, but to desire and seek, the face of God. Now, it is Christ who opens the door to us, yea, who is himself the door. (John 10:9.) As this is a double door thrown open for the admission both of Jews and Gentiles, we are led to view God as exhibiting to both his fatherly kindness. He adds,by one Spirit; who leads and guides us to Christ, and "by whom we cry, Abba, Father," (Romans 8:15,) for hence arises the boldness of approach. Jews had various means of drawing near to God; now all have but one way, to be led by the Spirit of God.

Verse 19

Now therefore ye are no more strangers. The Ephesians are now exclusively addressed. They were formerly strangers from the covenants of promise, but their condition was now changed. They were foreigners, but God had made them citizens of his church. The high value of that honor which God had been pleased to bestow upon them, is expressed in a variety of language. They are first called fellow-citizens with the saints, — next, of the household of God, — and lastly, stones properly fitted into the building of the temple of the Lord. The first appellation is taken from the comparison of the church to a state, which occurs very frequently in Scripture. Those who were formerly profane, and utterly unworthy to associate with godly persons, have been raised to distinguished honor in being admitted to be members of the same community with Abraham, — with all the holy patriarchs, and prophets, and kings, — nay, with the angels themselves. To be of the household of God, which is the second comparison, suggests equally exalted views of their present condition. God has admitted them into his own family; for the church is God's house.

Verse 20

And are built. The third comparison illustrates the manner in which the Ephesians, and all other Christians are admitted to the honor of being fellow-citizens with the saints and of the household of God. They are built on the foundation, — they are founded on the doctrine, of the apostles and prophets. We are thus enabled to distinguish between a true and a false church. This is of the greatest importance; for the tendency to error is always strong, and the consequences of mistake are dangerous in the extreme. No churches boast more loudly of the name than those which bear a false and empty title; as may be seen in our own times. To guard us against mistake, the mark of a true church is pointed out.

Foundation, in this passage, unquestionably means doctrine; for no mention is made of patriarchs or pious kings, but only of those who held the office of teachers, and whom God had appointed to superintend the edification of his church. It is laid down by Paul, that the faith of the church ought to be founded on this doctrine. What opinion, then, must we form of those who rest entirely on the contrivances of men, and yet accuse us of revolt, because we embrace the pure doctrine of God? But the manner in which it is founded deserves inquiry; for, in the strict sense of the term, Christ is the only foundation. He alone supports the whole church. He alone is the rule and standard of faith. But Christ is actually the foundation on which the church is built by the preaching of doctrine; and, on this account, the prophets and apostles are called builders. (1 Corinthians 3:10.) Nothing else, Paul tells us, was ever intended by the prophets and apostles, than to found a church on Christ.

We shall find this to be true, if we begin with Moses; for "Christ is the end of the law," (Romans 10:4,) and the sum of the gospel. Let us remember, therefore, that if we wish to be reckoned among believers, we must place our reliance on no other: if we wish to make sure progress in the knowledge of the Scriptures, to him our whole attention must be directed. The same lesson is taught, when we consult the word of God as contained in the writings of the prophets and apostles. To shew us how we ought to combine them, their harmony is pointed out; for they have a common foundation, and labor jointly in building the temple of God. Though the apostles have become our teachers, the instruction of the prophets has not been rendered superfluous; but one and the same object is promoted by both.

I have been led to make this remark by the conduct of the Marcionites in ancient times, who expunged the word prophets from this passage; and by that of certain fanatics in the present day, who, following their footsteps, exclaim loudly that we have nothing to do with the law and the prophets, because the gospel has put an end to their authority. The Holy Spirit everywhere declares, that he has spoken to us by the mouth of the prophets, and demands that we shall listen to him in their writings. This is of no small consequence for maintaining the authority of our faith. All the servants of God, from first to last, are so perfectly agreed, that their harmony is in itself a clear demonstration that it is one God who speaks in them all. The commencement of our religion must be traced to the creation of the world. In vain do Papists, Mahometans, and other sects, boast of their antiquity, while they are mere counterfeits of the true, the pure religion.

Jesus Christ, himself is the chief corner-stone (130) Those who transfer this honor to Peter, and maintain that on him the church is founded, are so void of shame, as to attempt to justify their error by quoting this passage. They hold out that Christ is called the chief corner-stone, by comparison with others; and that there are many stones on which the church is founded. But this difficulty is easily solved. Various metaphors are employed by the apostles according to the diversity of circumstances, but still with the same meaning. In writing to the Corinthians, Paul lays down an incontestable proposition, that "no other foundation can be laid." (1 Corinthians 3:11.)

He does not therefore mean, that Christ is merely a corner, or a part of the foundation; for then he would contradict himself. What then? He means that Jews and Gentiles were two separate walls, but are formed into one spiritual building. Christ is placed in the middle of the corner for the purpose of uniting both, and this is the force of the metaphor. What is immediately added shews sufficiently that he is very far from limiting Christ to any one part of the building.

Verse 21

In whom all the building groweth. If this be true, what will become of Peter? When Paul, in writing to the Corinthians, speaks of Christ as a "Foundation," he does not mean that the church is begun by him and completed by others, but draws a distinction arising out of a comparison of his own labors with those of other men. It had been his duty to found the church at Corinth, and to leave to his successors the completion of the building.

"According to the grace of God which is given to me, as a wise master-builder, I have laid the foundation, and another buildeth on it." (1 Corinthians 3:10.)

With respect to the present passage, he conveys the instruction, that all who are fitly framed together in Christ are the temple of the Lord. There is first required a fitting together, that believers may embrace and accommodate themselves to each other by mutual intercourse; otherwise there would not be a building, but a confused mass. The chief part of the symmetry consists in unity of faith. Next follows progress, or increase. Those who are not united in faith and love, so as to grow in the Lord, belong to a profane building, which has nothing in common with the temple of the Lord.

Groweth unto an holy temple. Individual believers are at other times called "temples of the Holy Ghost," (1 Corinthians 6:19; 2 Corinthians 6:16,) but here all are said to constitute one temple. In both cases the metaphor is just and appropriate. When God dwells in each of us, it is his will that we should embrace all in holy unity, and that thus he should form one temple out of many. Each person, when viewed separately, is a temple, but, when joined to others, becomes a stone of a temple; and this view is given for the sake of recommending the unity of the church.

Verse 22

In whom ye also are builded together, or in whom also Be Ye Builded together. The termination of the Greek verb , συνοικοδομεῖσθε, like that of the Latin, cooedificamini, does not enable us to determine whether it is in the imperative or indicative mood. The context will admit either, but I prefer the latter sense. It is, I think, an exhortation to the Ephesians to grow more and more in the faith of Christ, after having been once founded in it, and thus to form a part of that new temple of God, the building of which through the gospel was then in progress in every part of the world.

Through the Spirit. This is again repeated for two reasons: first, to remind them that all human exertions are of no avail without the operation of the Spirit; and secondly, to point out the superiority of the spiritual building to all Jewish and outward services.

CALVIN EPHESIANS 3

Verse 1

For this cause. Paul's imprisonment, which ought to have been held as a confirmation of his apostleship, was undoubtedly presented by his adversaries in an opposite light. He therefore points out to the Ephesians that his chains served to prove and to declare his calling; and that the only reason why he had been imprisoned was, that he had preached the gospel to the Gentiles. His unshaken firmness was no small additional proof that he had discharged his office in a proper manner.

The prisoner of Jesus Christ. (131) To strengthen his authority still more, he speaks in lofty terms of his prison. In the presence of the world and of wicked men, this might have appeared to be foolish boasting; but, in addressing godly persons, it was a dignified and faithful manner. The glory of Christ not only overcomes the ignominy of the chains, but converts what was in itself a reproach into the highest honor. If he had merely said, "I am a prisoner," this would not have conveyed the idea of his being an ambassador. Imprisonment alone has no claim to this honor, being usually the mark of wickedness and crime. But the crowns and sceptres of kings, to say nothing of the imposing splendor of an ambassador, are less honorable than the chains of a prisoner of Jesus Christ. Men might think otherwise, but it is our duty to judge of the reasons. So highly ought the name of Christ to be revered by us, that what men consider to be the greatest reproach, ought to be viewed by us as the greatest honour.

For you Gentiles. Another circumstance greatly fitted to interest the Ephesians was, that the persecutions of Paul were endured for the Gentiles, — that his troubles and dangers were on their account.

Verse 2

If ye have heard. There is reason to believe, that, while Paul was at Ephesus, he had said nothing on these subjects, no necessity for doing so having arisen; for no controversy had taken place among them about the calling of the Gentiles. If he had made any mention of them in his discourses, he would have reminded the Ephesians of his former statements, instead of referring generally, as he now does, to common report and to his own Epistle. He did not, of his own accord, raise unnecessary disputes. It was only when the wickedness of his adversaries made it necessary, that he reluctantly undertook the defense of his ministry. Dispensation (οικονομια) means here a divine order or command, or, as it is generally expressed, a commission.

Verse 3

That by revelation. Some might imagine, that, in attempting to discharge the office of an apostle, he had acted rashly, and was now paying the penalty of his rashness. It was this that made him so earnest in pleading the Divine authority for all his transactions. The present instance, on account of its novelty, had few supporters; and therefore he calls it a mystery. By this name he endeavors to remove the prejudice which the general displeasure at the event was fitted to excite. His own personal interest in the matter was less regarded than that of the Ephesians, who were deeply concerned in the information, that, through the settled purpose of God, they had been called by Paul's ministry. Lest what is little known should forthwith become the object of suspicion, the word mystery places it in opposition to the perverse judgments and opinions which were then prevalent in the world.

By revelation he made known to me the mystery. Paul draws the line of distinction between himself and those fanatics, who ascribe to God and to the Holy Spirit their own idle dreams. The false apostles boast of revelations, but it is a false boast. Paul was persuaded that his revelation was true, could prove it to others, and speaks of it as a fact of which no doubt could be entertained.

As I wrote a little before. This refers either to a rapid glance at the same subject in the second chapter, or — which appears to be the general opinion — to another Epistle. If the former exposition be adopted, it will be proper to translate, as I wrote before in few words; for the subject had received nothing more than a passing notice; but the latter being, as I have said, the prevailing opinion, I prefer translating, as I wrote a little before. The phrase, (ἐν ὀλίγῳ,) which Erasmus has translated in a few words, appears rather to refer to time. On this supposition there would be an implied comparison between the present and the former writings. But nothing would be more unlike the fact, than to contrast them on the score of brevity; for a more concise mode of expression than this passing glance can hardly be imagined. The phrase, a little before, seems purposely to be used as an appeal to their remembrance of a recent occurrence, though I do not insist on this point. There is more difficulty in the next verse.

Verse 4

By attending to which, ye may understand, πρὸς ὃ δύνασθε ἀναγινώσκοντες νοῶσαι. Erasmus renders it, "from which things, when ye read, ye may understand."

But to translate ἀναγινώσκειν τι as signifying to read is, I think, at variance with Greek syntax. I leave it as a subject of consideration, whether it does not rather signify to attend. The participle would then be connected with the preposition πρὸς, in the commencement of the verse, and the clause would run thus, to which when ye attend, ye may understand If, however, by viewing the verb ἀναγινώσκοντες, as disjoined from the preposition, you make it signify reading, the meaning will still be, "by reading you may understand according to what I have written;" taking the phrase πρὸς ὃ, to which, as equivalent to καθ ᾽ ὃ, according to which; but I suggest this merely as a doubtful conjecture.

If we adopt the view which is almost universally approved, that the apostle had formerly written to the Ephesians, this is not the only Epistle which we have lost. And yet there is no room for the sneers of the ungodly, as if the Scriptures had been mutilated, or in any part had become imperfect. If we duly consider Paul's earnestness, — his watchfulness and care, — his zeal and fervor, — his kindness and readiness in assisting brethren, — we shall be led to regard it as highly probable that he would write many epistles, both of a public and private nature, to various places. Those which the Lord judged to be necessary for his church have been selected by his providence for everlasting remembrance. Let us rest assured, that what is left is enough for us, and that the smallness of the remaining number is not the result of accident; but that the body of Scripture, which is in our possession, has been adjusted by the wonderful counsel of God.

My knowledge. The frequent mention of this point shews the necessity that the calling of ministers should be firmly believed both by themselves and by their people. But Paul looks more to others than to himself. He had everywhere indeed given great offense by preaching the gospel indiscriminately to Jews and Gentiles, but his solicitude was not chiefly on his own account. There were not a few who, overwhelmed by the slanders of wicked men, began to doubt of his apostleship, and whose faith was consequently shaken. It was this that induced him so frequently to remind the Ephesians that he knew the will and command of God who called him to the office. —In the mystery of Christ,

Verse 5

Which in other ages was not made known. He had simply called it a mystery, but now calls it a mystery of Christ, because it was necessary that it should remain hidden, until it was revealed by his coming; just as the appellation of "prophecies of Christ" may be given to those which relate to his kingdom. We must first explain the word mystery, and then inquire why it is said to have remained unknown in all ages. The mystery was,

"that the Gentiles should be fellow-heirs, and of the same body, and partakers of his promise in Christ by the gospel."
(Ephesians 3:6.)

When this name is given to the gospel, it has other meanings, which do not apply to the present passage. The calling of the Gentiles, then, was a "mystery of Christ;" that is, it was to be fulfilled under the reign of Christ.

But why does he affirm that it was not known, when it had been the subject of so many predictions? The prophets everywhere declare, that people shall come from every nation in the world, to worship God; that an altar shall be erected both in Assyria and in Egypt, and that all alike shall speak the language of Canaan. (Isaiah 19:18.) It is intimated by these words, that the worship of the true God, and the same profession of faith, will be everywhere diffused. Of the Messiah it is predicted, that he shall have dominion from east to west, and that all nations shall serve him. (Psalms 72:8.) We see also, that many passages to this purpose are quoted by the apostles, not only from the later prophets, but from Moses. How could that be hidden which had been proclaimed by so many heralds? Why are all without exception pronounced to have been in ignorance? Shall we say, that the prophets spake what they did not understand, and uttered sounds without meaning?

I answer, the words of Paul must not be understood to mean that there had been no knowledge at all on these subjects. There had always been some of the Jewish nation who acknowledged that, at the advent of the Messiah, the grace of God would be proclaimed throughout the whole world, and who looked forward to the renovation of the human race. The prophets themselves, though they spoke with the certainty of revelation, left the time and manner undetermined. They knew that some communication of the grace of God would be made to the Gentiles, but at what time, in what manner, and by what means it should be accomplished, they had no information whatever. This ignorance was exemplified in a remarkable way by the apostles. They had not only been instructed by the predictions of the prophets, but had heard the distinct statement of their Master, (John 10:16,)

"Other sheep I have which are not of this fold: them also I must bring, and they shall hear my voice: and there shall be one fold and one shepherd;"

and yet the novelty of the subject prevented them from understanding it fully. Nay, after they had received the injunction,

"Go ye into all the world, and preach the gospel to every creature," (Mark 16:15,)

and,

"Ye shall be witnesses to me both in Jerusalem, and in all Judea, and in Samaria, and to the uttermost part of the earth," (Acts 1:8,)

they dreaded and recoiled from the calling of the Gentiles as a proposal absolutely monstrous, because the manner of its accomplishment was still unknown. Before the actual event arrived, they had dark and confused apprehensions of our Savior's words; for ceremonies were

"a vail over their face, that they could not steadfastly look to the end of that which is abolished." (2 Corinthians 3:13.)

With unquestionable propriety, therefore, does Paul call this a mystery, and say, that it had been hidden; for the repeal of the ceremonial law, which admitted them within the vail, was not understood.

As it is now revealed. To lay claim to information which none of the patriarchs, prophets, or holy kings, had possessed, might wear the aspect of arrogance. To guard against this imputation, Paul reminds them, first, that in this respect he was not alone, but shared the revelation with the most eminent teachers of the church; and, secondly, that it was the gift of the Holy Spirit, who has a right to bestow it on whom he pleases; for there is no other limit of our knowledge but that which he assigns to us.

These few words, as it is now revealed, throw additional light on the admission of the Gentiles to be the people of God. It is on the condition that they shall be placed on a level with the Jews, and form one body. That the novelty might give no offense, he states that this must be accomplished by the gospel. (Ephesians 3:6.) Now, the gospel was itself a novelty; for it had never till now been heard of, and yet was acknowledged by all the godly to have come from heaven. Where, then, was the wonder, if, in renewing the world, God should follow an unwonted method?

Verse 7

Of which I was made a minister. Having declared the gospel to be the instrument employed in communicating grace to the Gentiles, he now adds, that he was made a minister of the Gospel; and thus applies to himself the general statements which had been made. But, to avoid claiming for himself more than is proper, he affirms that it isthe gift of the grace of God, and that this gift was an exhibition of divine power. As if he had said, "Inquire not what I have deserved; for in the free exercise of kindness, the Lord made me an apostle of the Gentiles, not for any excellence of mine, but by his own grace. Inquire not what I formerly was; for it is the Lord's prerogative to 'exalt them of low degree.'" (Luke 1:52.) To produce something great out of nothing, shews the effectual working of his power.

Verse 8

To me, who am the least. He labors to exhibit himself, and everything that belongs to him, in as humiliating a light as possible, in order that the grace of God may be the more highly exalted. But this acknowledgment had the additional effect of anticipating the objections which his adversaries might bring against him. "Who is this man that God should have raised him above all his brethren? What superior excellence did he possess that he should be chosen in preference to all the others?" All such comparisons of personal worth are set aside by the confession, that he wasthe least of all the saints.

This is no hypocritical declaration. Most men are ready enough to make professions of feigned humility, while their minds are swelled with pride, and in words to acknowledge themselves inferior to every one else, while they wish to be regarded with the highest esteem, and think themselves entitled to the highest honor. Paul is perfectly sincere in admitting his unworthiness; nay, at other times he speaks of himself in far more degrading language.

"For I am the least of the apostles, and am not worthy to be called an apostle, because I persecuted the church of God."
(1 Corinthians 15:9.)

"Christ Jesus came into the world to save sinners, of whom I am chief "
(1 Timothy 1:15.)

But let us observe, that, when he speaks of himself as the meanest of all, he confines his attention to what he was in himself, apart from the grace of God. As if he had said, that his own worthlessness did not prevent him from being appointed, while others were passed by, to be the apostle of the Gentiles. The grace of God given to me is the expression used by him, to intimate that it was a peculiar gift, as compared with what had been bestowed on others. Not that he alone had been elected to discharge that office, but that he held the highest rank among "the teachers of the Gentiles," — a title which he employs on another occasion as peculiar to himself.

"I am ordained a preacher, and an apostle, (I speak the truth in Christ, and lie not,) a teacher of the Gentiles in faith and truth."
(1 Timothy 2:7.)

By the unsearchable riches of Christ are meant the astonishing and boundless treasures of grace, which God had suddenly and unexpectedly bestowed on the Gentiles. The Ephesians are thus reminded how eagerly the gospel ought to be embraced, and how highly it ought to be esteemed. This subject has been treated in the Exposition of the Epistle to the Galatians, (Galatians 1:15.) And certainly, while Paul held the office of apostleship in common with others, it was an honor peculiar to himself to be appointed apostle of the Gentiles.

Verse 9

What is the fellowship of the mystery. The publication of the gospel is called a fellowship, because it is the will of God that his purpose, which had formerly been hidden, shall now be shared by men. There is an appropriate metaphor in the words φωτίσαι πάντας, to enlighten all men, — conveying the thought, that, in his apostleship, the grace of God shines with the brightness of noon-day.

Which hath been hid in God. This is intended, as before, to obviate the prejudice of novelty, — to oppose the rashness of men, who think it improper that they should remain in ignorance of anything whatever. Who will question the right which God has to keep his own purposes concealed, until he shall be pleased to communicate them to men? What presumption, — yea, what madness is it, not to admit that God is wiser than we! Let us remember, therefore, that our rashness ought to receive a check, whenever the boundless height of the Divine foreknowledge is presented to our view. This, too, is the reason why he calls them the unsearchable riches of Christ; intimating that this subject, though it exceeds our capacity, ought to be contemplated with reverence and admiration.

Who created all things by Jesus Christ. This cannot so properly be understood of the first creation as of the spiritual renewal. It is, no doubt, true, and is frequently declared in Scripture, that by the Word of God all things were created; but the connection of the passage lays us under the necessity of understanding by it that renewal which is comprehended in the blessing of redemption. But it may, perhaps, be thought that the apostle is illustrating this renewal, by an argument drawn from the creation. "By Christ, as God, the Father created (John 1:3) all things; and why, then, should we wonder, if by Christ, as Mediator, all the Gentiles are now brought back to one body?" I have no objection to this view. A similar argument is used by him in another Epistle.

"For God, who commanded the light to shine out of darkness, is the same who hath shined in our hearts, to give the light of the knowledge of the glory of God in the face of Jesus Christ."
(2 Corinthians 4:6.)

From the creation of the world he concludes, that it is the work of God to enlighten the darkness; but what was visible in the former case is ascribed to the Spirit, when he comes to speak of the kingdom of Christ.

Verse 10

That now to the principalities and powers. Some are of opinion that these words cannot apply to angels, because such ignorance, as is here supposed, could not be found in those who are permitted to behold the brightness of God's countenance. They choose rather to refer them to devils, but without due reflection; for what could have been regarded as extraordinary in the assertion, that, by the preaching of the gospel and the calling of the Gentiles, information was, for the first time, conveyed to devils? There can be no doubt that the apostle labors to place in the strongest light the mercy of God toward the Gentiles, and the high value of the gospel. For this purpose he declares, that the preaching of the gospel exhibits the manifold grace of God, with which, till now, the heavenly angels themselves were unacquainted. The wisdom of God, therefore, which was manifested by uniting Jews and Gentiles in the fellowship of the gospel, ought to be regarded by men with the highest admiration.

He calls it πολυποίκιλον σοφίαν, manifold wisdom, because men are accustomed to try it by a false standard, confining their view to a particular department, and thus forming a most inadequate conception of the whole. The Jews thought, for example, that the dispensation under the law, with which they were acquainted and familiar, was the only form in which the wisdom of God could be seen. But, by making the gospel to be proclaimed to all men without exception, God has brought forth to view another instance and proof of his wisdom. Not that it was new wisdom, but that it was so large and manifold, (132) as to transcend our limited capacity. Let us rest assured that the knowledge, whatever it may be, which we have acquired, is, after all, but a slender proportion. And if the calling of the Gentiles draws the attention, and excites the reverence, of angels in heaven, how shameful that it should be slighted or disdained by men upon earth!

The inference which some draw from this passage, that angels are present in our assemblies, and make progress along with ourselves in knowledge, is a groundless speculation. We must always keep in view the purposes for which God appointed the ministry of his word. If angels, who are permitted to see the face of God, do not walk in faith, neither do they need the outward administration of the word. The preaching of the gospel, therefore, is of no service but to human beings, among whom alone the practice exists. Paul's meaning is this: "The church, composed both of Jews and Gentiles, is a mirror, in which angels behold the astonishing wisdom of God displayed in a manner unknown to them before. They see a work which is new to them, and the reason of which was hid in God. In this manner, and not by learning anything from the lips of men, do they make progress."

Verse 11

According to the eternal purpose. How carefully does he guard against the objection, that the purpose of God has been changed! A third time, he repeats that the decree was eternal and unchangeable, but must be carried into effect by Christ Jesus our Lord, because in him it was made. Thus he declares, that the proper time for publishing this decree belongs to the kingdom of Christ. Literally the words run, "according to the eternal purpose (ἣν ἐποίησοεν) which he made. " But I consider the meaning to be, which he purposed; because the present discussion does not relate solely to the execution of the decree, but to the appointment itself, which, though it took place before all ages, was known to God only — till the manifestation of Christ.

Verse 12

Through whom we have boldness. The honor of reconciling the Father to the whole world must be given to Christ. From the effects of this grace its excellence is demonstrated; for faith, which is possessed by Gentiles in common with Jews, admits them into the presence of God. When the words, through Christ and by the faith of him, are used by Paul, in connection with the name of God, there is always an implied contrast, which shuts up every other approach, — which excludes every other method of obtaining Divine fellowship. Most important and valuable instruction is here conveyed. The true nature and power of faith, and the confidence which is necessary for calling upon God, are beautifully expressed. That the consequences of faith, and the duties which it performs, should be the subject of much controversy between us and the Papists, is not surprising. They do not properly understand the meaning of the word Faith, which they might learn from this passage, if they were not blinded by prejudice.

First, Paul denominates it the faith of Christ; by which he intimates, that everything which faith ought to contemplate is exhibited to us in Christ. Hence it follows, that an empty and confused knowledge of Christ must not be mistaken for Faith, but that knowledge which is directed to Christ, in order to seek God in Christ; and this can only be done when the power and offices of Christ are understood.Faith producesconfidence, which again, in its turn, produces boldness. There are three stages in our progress. First, we believe the promises of God; next, by relying on them, we obtain that confidence, which is accompanied by holiness and peace of mind; and, last of all, comes boldness, which enables us to banish fear, and to come with firmness and steadiness into the presence of God.

To separate faith from confidence would be an attempt to take away heat and light from the sun. I acknowledge, indeed, that, in proportion to the measure of faith, confidence is small in some and greater in others; but faith will never be found unaccompanied by these effects or fruits. A trembling, hesitating, doubting conscience, will always be a sure evidence of unbelief; but a firm, steady faith, will prove to be invincible against the gates of hell. To trust in Christ as Mediator, and to entertain a firm conviction of our heavenly Father's love, — to venture boldly to promise to ourselves eternal life, and not to tremble at death or hell, — is, to use a common phrase, a holy presumption.

Observe the expression, access with confidence. Wicked men seek rest in forgetfulness of God, and are never at ease but when they remove to the greatest possible distance from God. His own children differ from them in this respect, that they "have peace with God," (Romans 5:1,) and approach to him with cheerfulness and delight. We infer, likewise, from this passage, that, in order to call on God in a proper manner, confidence is necessary, and thus becomes the key that opens to us the gate of heaven. Those who doubt and hesitate will never be heard.

"Let him ask in faith," says James, "nothing wavering: for he that wavereth is like a wave of the sea driven with the wind and tossed. For let not that man think that he shall receive anything of the Lord." (James 1:6)

The sophists of the Sorbonne, (133) when they enjoin men to hesitate, know not what it is to call upon God.

Verse 13

Wherefore I desire. His reason for alluding formerly to his imprisonment is now manifest. It was to prevent them from being discouraged when they heard of his persecution. (134) O heroic breast, which drew from a prison, and from death itself, comfort to those who were not in danger! He says that, he endured tribulations for the Ephesians, because they tended to promote the edification of all the godly. How powerfully is the faith of the people confirmed, when a pastor does not hesitate to seal his doctrine by the surrender of his life! And accordingly he adds, which is your glory. Such lustre was thrown around his instructions, that all the churches among whom he had labored, had good reason to glory, when they beheld their faith ratified by the best of all pledges.

Verse 14

For this cause. His prayers for them are mentioned, not only to testify his regard for them, but likewise to excite them to pray in the same manner; for the seed of the word is scattered in vain, unless the Lord render it fruitful by his blessing. Let pastors learn from Paul's example, not only to admonish and exhort their people, but to entreat the Lord to bless their labors, that they may not be unfruitful. Nothing will be gained by their industry and toil, — all their study and application will be to no purpose, except so far as the Lord bestows his blessing. This ought not to be regarded by them as an encouragement to sloth. It is their duty, on the contrary, to labor earnestly in sowing and watering, provided they, at the same time, ask and expect the increase from the Lord.

We are thus enabled to refute the slanders of the Pelagians and Papists, who argue, that, if the grace of the Holy Spirit performs the whole work of enlightening our minds, and forming our hearts to obedience, all instruction will be superfluous. The only effect of the enlightening and renewing influences of the Holy Spirit is, to give to instruction its proper weight and efficacy, that we may not be blind to the light of heaven, or deaf to the strains of truth. While the Lord alone acts upon us, he acts by his own instruments. It is therefore the duty of pastors diligently to teach, — of the people, earnestly to receive instruction, — and of both, not to weary themselves in unprofitable exertions, but to look up for Divine aid.

I bow my knees. The bodily attitude is here put for the religious exercise itself. Not that prayer, in all cases, requires the bending of the knees, but because this expression of reverence is commonly employed, especially where it is not an incidental petition, but a continued prayer.

Verse 15

Of whom the whole family. (135) The relative , ἐξ οὗ, of whom, may apply equally to the Father and to the Son. Erasmus restricts it entirely to the Father. I do not approve of this; for readers ought to have been allowed a liberty of choice; nay, the other interpretation appears to be far more probable. The apostle alludes to that relationship which the Jews had with each other, through their father Abraham, to whom they trace their lineage. He proposes, on the contrary, to remove the distinction between Jews and Gentiles; and tells them, not only that all men have been brought into one family and one race through Christ, but that they are enabled to claim kindred even with angels.

To apply it to God the Father would not be equally defensible, being liable to this obvious exception, that God formerly passed by the Gentiles, and adopted the Jews as his peculiar people. But when we apply it to Christ, the whole of Paul's statement agrees with the facts; for all come and blend together, as one family, and, related to one God the Father, are mutually brethren. Let us therefore understand that, through the mediation of Christ, a relationship has been constituted between Jews and Gentiles, because, by reconciling us to the Father, he has made us all one. Jews have no longer any reason to boast that they are the posterity of Abraham, or that they belong to this or that tribe, — to despise others as profane, and claim the exclusive honor of being a holy people. There is but one relationship which ought to be reckoned, both in heaven and on earth, both among angels and among men — a union to the body of Christ. Out of him all will be found scattered. He alone is the bond by which we are united.

Verse 16

That he would give to you. Paul wishes that the Ephesians should be strengthened; and yet he had already bestowed on their piety no mean commendation. But believers have never advanced so far as not to need farther growth. The highest perfection of the godly in this life is an earnest desire to make progress. This strengthening, he tells us, is the work of the Spirit; so that it does not proceed from man's own ability. The increase, as well as the commencement, of everything good in us, comes from the Holy Spirit. That it is the gift of Divine grace, is evident from the expression used, that he would give to you This the Papists utterly deny. They maintain that the second grace is bestowed upon us, according as we have individually deserved it, by making a proper use of the first grace. But let us unite with Paul in acknowledging that it is the "gift" of the grace of God, not only that we have begun to run well, but that we advance; not only that we have been born again, but that we grow from day to day.

According to the riches of his glory. These words are intended to express still more strongly the doctrine of Divine grace. They may be explained in two ways: either, according to his glorious riches, making the genitive, agreeably to the Hebrew idiom, supply the place of an adjective, — or, according to his rich and abundant glory. The word glory will thus be put for mercy, in accordance with an expression which he had formerly used, "to the praise of the glory of his grace." (Ephesians 1:6) I prefer the latter view.

In the inner man. By the inner man, Paul means the soul, and whatever relates to the spiritual life of the soul; as the outward man denotes the body, with everything that belongs to it, — health, honors, riches, vigor, beauty, and everything of that nature. "Though our outward man perish, yet our inward man is renewed day by day;" that is, if in worldly matters we decay, our spiritual life becomes more and more vigorous. (2 Corinthians 4:16) The prayer of Paul, that the saints may be strengthened, does not mean that they may be eminent and flourishing in the world, but that, with respect to the kingdom of God, their minds may be made strong by Divine power.

Verse 17

That Christ may dwell. He explains what is meant by "the strength of the inner man." As

"it pleased the Father that in him should all fullness dwell," (Colossians 1:19,)

so he who has Christ dwelling in him can want nothing. It is a mistake to imagine that the Spirit can be obtained without obtaining Christ; and it is equally foolish and absurd to dream that we can receive Christ without the Spirit. Both doctrines must be believed. We are partakers of the Holy Spirit, in proportion to the intercourse which we maintain with Christ; for the Spirit will be found nowhere but in Christ, on whom he is said, on that account, to have rested; for he himself says, by the prophet Isaiah, "The Spirit of the Lord God is upon me." (Isaiah 61:1; Luke 4:18.) But neither can Christ be separated from his Spirit; for then he would be said to be dead, and to have lost all his power.

Justly, therefore, does Paul affirm that the persons who are endowed by God with spiritual vigor are those in whom Christ dwells. He points to that part in which Christ peculiarly dwells,in your hearts, — to show that it is not enough if the knowledge of Christ dwell on the tongue or flutter in the brain.

May dwell through faith. The method by which so great a benefit is obtained is also expressed. What a remarkable commendation is here bestowed on faith, that, by means of it, the Son of God becomes our own, and "makes his abode with us!" (John 14:23.) By faith we not only acknowledge that Christ suffered and rose from the dead on our account, but, accepting the offers which he makes of himself, we possess and enjoy him as our Savior. This deserves our careful attention. Most people consider fellowship with Christ, and believing in Christ, to be the same thing; but the fellowship which we have with Christ is the consequence of faith. In a word, faith is not a distant view, but a warm embrace, of Christ, by which he dwells in us, and we are filled with the Divine Spirit.

That ye may be rooted and grounded in love. Among the fruits of Christ's dwelling in us the apostle enumerates love and gratitude for the Divine grace and kindness exhibited to us in Christ. Hence it follows, that this is true and solid excellence; so that, whenever he treats of the perfection of the saints, he views it as consisting of these two parts. The firmness and constancy which our love ought to possess are pointed out by two metaphors. There are many persons not wholly destitute of love; but it is easily removed or shaken, because its roots are not deep. Paul desires that it should berooted (136) and grounded, — thoroughly fixed in our minds, so as to resemble a well-founded building or deeply-planted tree. The true meaning is, that our roots ought to be so deeply planted, and our foundation so firmly laid in love, that nothing will be able to shake us. It is idle to infer from these words, that love is the foundation and root of our salvation. Paul does not inquire here, as any one may perceive, on what our salvation is founded, but with what firmness and constancy we ought to continue in the exercise of love.

Verse 18

May be able to comprehend. The second fruit is, that the Ephesians should perceive the greatness of Christ's love to men. Such an apprehension or knowledge springs from faith. By desiring that they should comprehend it with all saints, he shows that it is the most excellent blessing which they can obtain in the present life; that it is the highest wisdom, to which all the children of God aspire. What follows is sufficiently clear in itself, but has hitherto been darkened by a variety of interpretations. Augustine is quite delighted with his own acuteness, which throws no light on the subject. Endeavouring to discover some kind of mysterious allusion to the figure of the cross, he makes the breadth to be love, — the height, hope, — the length, patience, and the depth, humility. This is very ingenious and entertaining: but what has it to do with Paul's meaning? Not more, certainly, than the opinion of Ambrose, that the allusion is to the figure of a sphere. Laying aside the views of others, I shall state what will be universally acknowledged to be the simple and true meaning.

Verse 19

And to know the love of Christ. By those dimensions Paul means nothing else than the love of Christ, of which he speaks afterwards. The meaning is, that he who knows it fully and perfectly is in every respect a wise man. As if he had said, "In whatever direction men may look, they will find nothing in the doctrine of salvation that does not bear some relation to this subject." The love of Christ contains within itself the whole of wisdom, so that the words may run thus: that ye may be able to comprehend the love of Christ, which is the length and breadth, and depth, and height, that is, the complete perfection of all wisdom. The metaphor is borrowed from mathematicians, taking the parts as expressive of the whole. Almost all men are infected with the disease of desiring to obtain useless knowledge. It is of great importance that we should be told what is necessary for us to know, and what the Lord desires us to contemplate, above and below, on the right hand and on the left, before and behind. The love of Christ is held out to us as the subject which ought to occupy our daily and nightly meditations, and in which we ought to be wholly plunged. He who is in possession of this alone has enough. Beyond it there is nothing solid, nothing useful, — nothing, in short, that is proper or sound. Though you survey the heaven and earth and sea, you will never go beyond this without overstepping the lawful boundary of wisdom.

Which surpasseth knowledge. A similar expression occurs in another Epistle:

"the peace of God, which surpasseth all understanding, shall keep your hearts and minds through Christ Jesus."
(Philippians 4:7)

No man can approach to God without being raised above himself and above the world. On this ground the sophists refuse to admit that we can know with certainty that we enjoy the grace of God; for they measure faith by the perception of the bodily senses. But Paul justly contends that this wisdom exceeds all knowledge; for, if the faculties of man could reach it, the prayer of Paul that God would bestow it must have been unnecessary. Let us remember, therefore, that the certainty of faith is knowledge, but is acquired by the teaching of the Holy Spirit, not by the acuteness of our own intellect. If the reader desire a more full discussion of this subject, he may consult the "Institutes of the Christian Religion."

That ye may be filled. Paul now expresses in one word what he meant by the various dimensions. He who has Christ has everything necessary for being made perfect in God; for this is the meaning of the phrase, the fullness of God. Men do certainly imagine that they have entire completeness in themselves, but it is only when their pride is swelled with empty trifles. It is a foolish and wicked dream, that by the fullness of God is meant the full Godhead, as if men were raised to an equality with God.

Verse 20

Now to him. He now breaks out into thanksgiving, which serves the additional purpose of exhorting the Ephesians to maintain "good hope through grace," (2 Thessalonians 2:16,) and to endeavor constantly to obtain more and more adequate conceptions of the value of the grace of God.

Who is able. (137) This refers to the future, and agrees with what we are taught concerning hope; and indeed we cannot offer to God proper or sincere thanksgivings for favors received, unless we are convinced that his goodness to us will be without end. When he says that God is able, he does not mean power viewed apart, as the phrase is, from the act, but power which is exerted, and which we actually feel. Believers ought always to connect it with the work, when the promises made to them, and their own salvation, form the subject of inquiry. Whatever God can do, he unquestionably will do, if he has promised it. This the apostle proves both by former instances, and by the efficacy of the Spirit, which was at this very time exerted on their own minds.

According to the power that worketh in us, — according to what we feel within ourselves; for every benefit which God bestows upon us is a manifestation of his grace, and love, and power, in consequence of which we ought to cherish a stronger confidence for the future. Exceeding abundantly above all that we ask or think, is a remarkable expression, and bids us entertain no fear lest faith of a proper kind should go to excess. Whatever expectations we form of Divine blessings, the infinite goodness of God will exceed all our wishes and all our thoughts.

CALVIN EPHESIANS 4

Verse 1

The three remaining chapters consist entirely of practical exhortations. Mutual agreement is the first subject, in the course of which a discussion is introduced respecting the government of the church, as having been framed by our Lord for the purpose of maintaining unity among Christians.

I therefore, the prisoner of the Lord. His imprisonment, which might have been supposed more likely to render him despised, is appealed to, as we have already seen, for a confirmation of his authority. It was the seal of that embassy with which he had been honored. Whatever belongs to Christ, though in the eyes of men it may be attended by ignominy, ought to be viewed by us with the highest regard. The apostle's prison is more truly venerable than the splendid retinue or triumphal chariot of kings.

That ye may walk worthy. This is a general sentiment, a sort of preface, on which all the following statements are founded. He had formerly illustrated the calling with which they were called, (138) and now reminds them that they must live in obedience to God, in order that they may not be unworthy of such distinguished grace.

Verse 2

With all humility. He now descends to particulars, and first of all he mentions humility The reason is, that he was about to enter on the subject of Unity, to which humility is the first step. This again produces meekness, which disposes us to bear with our brethren, and thus to preserve that unity which would otherwise be broken a hundred times in a day. Let us remember, therefore, that, in cultivating brotherly kindness, we must begin with humility. Whence come rudeness, pride, and disdainful language towards brethren? Whence come quarrels, insults, and reproaches? Come they not from this, that every one carries his love of himself, and his regard to his own interests, to excess? By laying aside haughtiness and a desire of pleasing ourselves, we shall become meek and gentle, and acquire that moderation of temper which will overlook and forgive many things in the conduct of our brethren. Let us carefully observe the order and arrangement of these exhortations. It will be to no purpose that we inculcate forbearance till the natural fierceness has been subdued, and mildness acquired; and it will be equally vain to discourse of meekness, till we have begun with humility.

Forbearing one another in love. This agrees with what is elsewhere taught, that "love suffereth long and is kind." (1 Corinthians 13:4.) Where love is strong and prevalent, we shall perform many acts of mutual forbearance.

Verse 3

Endeavoring to keep the unity of the Spirit. With good reason does he recommend forbearance, as tending to promote the unity of the Spirit. Innumerable offenses arise daily, which might produce quarrels, particularly when we consider the extreme bitterness of man's natural temper. Some consider the unity of the Spirit to mean that spiritual unity which is produced in us by the Spirit of God. There can be no doubt that He alone makes us "of one accord, of one mind," (Philippians 2:2,) and thus makes us one; but I think it more natural to understand the words as denoting harmony of views. This unity, he tells us, is maintained by the bond of peace; for disputes frequently give rise to hatred and resentment. We must live at peace, if we would wish that brotherly kindness should be permanent amongst us.

Verse 4

There is one body. (139) He proceeds to show more fully in how complete a manner Christians ought to be united. The union ought to be such that we shall form one body and one soul. These words denote the whole man. We ought to be united, not in part only, but in body and soul. He supports this by a powerful argument, as ye have been called in one hope of your calling. We are called to one inheritance and one life; and hence it follows, that we cannot obtain eternal life without living in mutual harmony in this world. One Divine invitation being addressed to all, they ought to be united in the same profession of faith, and to render every kind of assistance to each other. Oh, were this thought deeply impressed upon our minds, that we are subject to a law which no more permits the children of God to differ among themselves than the kingdom of heaven to be divided, how earnestly should we cultivate brotherly kindness! How should we dread every kind of animosity, if we duly reflected that all who separate us from brethren, estrange us from the kingdom of God! And yet, strangely enough, while we forget the duties which brethren owe to each other, we go on boasting that we are the sons of God. Let us learn from Paul, that none are at all fit for that inheritance who are not one body and one spirit.

Verse 5

One Lord. In the first Epistle to the Corinthians, he employs the word Lord, to denote simply the government of God.

"There are differences of administration, but the same Lord."
(1 Corinthians 12:5)

In the present instance, as he shortly afterwards makes express mention of the Father, he gives this appellation strictly to Christ, who has been appointed by the Father to be our Lord, and to whose government we cannot be subject, unless we are of one mind. The frequent repetition of the word one is emphatic. Christ cannot be divided. Faith cannot be rent. There are not various baptisms, but one which is common to all. God cannot cease to be one, and unchangeable. It cannot but be our duty to cherish holy unity, which is bound by so many ties. Faith, and baptism, and God the Father, and Christ, ought to unite us, so as almost to become one man. All these arguments for unity deserve to be pondered, but cannot be fully explained. I reckon it enough to take a rapid glance at the apostle's meaning, leaving the full illustration of it to the preachers of the gospel. The unity of faith, which is here mentioned, depends on the one, eternal truth of God, on which it is founded.

One baptism, This does not mean that Christian baptism is not to be administered more than once, but that one baptism is common to all; so that, by means of it, we begin to form one body and one soul. But if that argument has any force, a much stronger one will be founded on the truth, that the Father, and Son, and Spirit, are one God; for it is one baptism, which is celebrated in the name of the Three Persons. What reply will the Arians or Sabellians make to this argument? Baptism possesses such force as to make us one; and in baptism, the name of the Father, and of the Son, and of the Spirit, is invoked. Will they deny that one Godhead is the foundation of this holy and mysterious unity? We are compelled to acknowledge, that the ordinance of baptism proves the existence of Three Persons in one Divine essence.

Verse 6

One God and Father of all. This is the main argument, from which all the rest flow. How comes it that we are united by faith, by baptism, or even by the government of Christ, but because God the Father, extending to each of us his gracious presence, employs these means for gathering us to himself? The two phrases , ἐπὶ πάντων καὶ διὰ πάντων, may either mean, above all and through all Things, or above all and through all Men. Either meaning will apply sufficiently well, or rather, in both cases, the meaning will be the same. Although God by his power upholds, and maintains, and rules, all things, yet Paul is not now speaking of the universal, but of the spiritual government which belongs to the church. By the Spirit of sanctification, God spreads himself through all the members of the church, embraces all in his government, and dwells in all; but God is not inconsistent with himself, and therefore we cannot but be united to him into one body.

This spiritual unity is mentioned by our Lord.

"Holy Father, keep through thine own name those whom thou hast, given me, that they may be one as we are."
(John 17:11)

This is true indeed, in a general sense, not only of all men but of all creatures. "In him we live, and move, and have our being." (Acts 17:28.) And again, "Do not I fill heaven and earth, saith the Lord?" (Jeremiah 23:24.) But we must attend to the connection in which this passage stands. Paul is now illustrating the mutual relation of believers, which has nothing in common either with wicked men or with inferior animals. To this relation we must limit what is said about God's government and presence. It is for this reason, also, that the apostle uses the word Father, which applies only to the members of Christ.

Verse 7

But to every one. He now describes the manner in which God establishes and preserves among us a mutual relation. No member of the body of Christ is endowed with such perfection as to be able, without the assistance of others, to supply his own necessities. A certain proportion is allotted to each; and it is only by communicating with each other, that all enjoy what is sufficient for maintaining their respective places in the body. The diversity of gifts is discussed in another Epistle, and very nearly with the same object.

"There are diversities of gifts, but the same Spirit"
(1 Corinthians 12:4.)

Such a diversity, we are there taught, is so far from injuring, that it tends to promote and strengthen, the harmony of believers.

The meaning of this verse may be thus summed up. "On no one has God bestowed all things. Each has received a certain measure. Being thus dependent on each other, they find it necessary to throw their individual gifts into the common stock, and thus to render mutual aid." The words grace and gift remind us that, whatever may be our attainments, we ought not to be proud of them, because they lay us under deeper obligations to God. These blessings are said to be the gift of Christ; for, as the apostle, first of all, mentioned the Father, so his aim, as we shall see, is to represent all that we are, and all that we have, as gathered together in Christ.

Verse 8

Therefore he saith. To serve the purpose of his argument, Paul has departed not a little from the true meaning of this quotation. Wicked men charge him with having made an unfair use of Scripture. The Jews go still farther, and, for the sake of giving to their accusations a greater air of plausibility, maliciously pervert the natural meaning of this passage. What is said of God, is applied by them to David or to the people. "David, or the people," they say, "ascended on high, when, in consequence of many victories, they rose superior to their enemies." But a careful examination of the Psalm will convince any reader that the words, he ascended up on high, are applied strictly to God alone.

The whole Psalm may be regarded as an ἐπίνικιον, a song of triumph, which David sings to God on account of the victories which he had obtained; but, taking occasion from the narrative of his own exploits, he makes a passing survey of the astonishing deliverances which the Lord had formerly wrought for his people. His object is to shew, that we ought to contemplate in the history of the Church the glorious power and goodness of God; and among other things he says, Thou hast ascended on high. (Psalms 68:18.) The flesh is apt to imagine that God remains idle and asleep, when he does not openly execute his judgments. To the view of men, when the Church is oppressed, God is in some manner humbled; but, when he stretches out his avenging arm for her deliverance, he then appears to rouse himself, and to ascend his throne of judgment.

"Then the Lord awaked as one out of sleep, and like a mighty man that shouteth by reason of wine. And he smote his enemies in the hinder parts; he put them to a perpetual reproach."
(Psalms 78:65.)

This mode of expression is sufficiently common and familiar; and, in short, the deliverance of the Church is here called the ascension of God.

Perceiving that it is a song of triumph, in which David celebrates all the victories which God had wrought for the salvation of his Church, Paul very properly quoted the account given of God's ascension, and applied it to the person of Christ. The noblest triumph which God ever gained was when Christ, after subduing sin, conquering death, and putting Satan to flight, rose majestically to heaven, that he might exercise his glorious reign over the Church. Hitherto there is no ground for the objection, that Paul has applied this quotation in a manner inconsistent with the design of the Psalmist. The continued existence of the Church is represented by David to be a manifestation of the Divine glory. But no ascension of God more triumphant or memorable will ever occur, than that which took place when Christ was carried up to the right hand of the Father, that he might rule over all authorities and powers, and might become the everlasting guardian and protector of his people.

He led captivity captive. Captivity is a collective noun for captive enemies; and the plain meaning is, that God reduced his enemies to subjection, which was more fully accomplished in Christ than in any other way. He has not only gained a complete victory over the devil, and sin, and death, and all the power of hell, — but out of rebels he forms every day "a willing people," (Psalms 110:3,) when he subdues by his word the obstinacy of our flesh. On the other hand, his enemies — to which class all wicked men belong — are held bound by chains of iron, and are restrained by his power from exerting their fury beyond the limits which he shall assign.

And gave gifts to men. There is rather more difficulty in this clause; for the words of the Psalm are, "thou hast received gifts for men," while the apostle changes this expression into gave gifts, and thus appears to exhibit an opposite meaning. Still there is no absurdity here; for Paul does not always quote the exact words of Scripture, but, after referring to the passage, satisfies himself with conveying the substance of it in his own language. Now, it is clear that the gifts which David mentions were not received by God for himself, but for his people; and accordingly we are told, in an earlier part of the Psalm, that "the spoil" had been "divided" among the families of Israel. (Psalms 68:12.) Since therefore the intention of receiving was to give gifts, Paul can hardly be said to have departed from the substance, whatever alteration there may be in the words.

At the same time, I am inclined to a different opinion, that Paul purposely changed the word, and employed it, not as taken out of the Psalm, but as an expression of his own, adapted to the present occasion. Having quoted from the Psalm a few words descriptive of Christ's ascension, he adds, in his own language, and gave gifts, — for the purpose of drawing a comparison between the greater and the less. Paul intends to shew, that this ascension of God in the person of Christ was far more illustrious than the ancient triumphs of the Church; because it is a more honorable distinction for a conqueror to dispense his bounty largely to all classes, than to gather spoils from the vanquished.

The interpretation given by some, that Christ received from the Father what he would distribute to us, is forced, and utterly at variance with the apostle's purpose.

No solution of the difficulty, in my opinion, is more natural than this. Having made a brief quotation from the Psalm, Paul took the liberty of adding a statement, which, though not contained in the Psalm, is true in reference to Christ — a statement, too, by which the ascension of Christ is proved to be more illustrious, and more worthy of admiration, than those ancient manifestations of the Divine glory which David enumerates.

Verse 9

Now that he ascended. Here again the slanderers exclaim, that Paul's reasoning is trifling and childish. "Why does he attempt to make those words apply to a real ascension of Christ, which were figuratively spoken about a manifestation of the Divine glory? Who does not know that the word ascend is metaphorical? The conclusion, that he also descended first, has therefore no weight."

I answer, Paul does not here reason in the manner of a logician, as to what necessarily follows, or may be inferred, from the words of the prophet. He knew that what David spake about God's ascension was metaphorical. But neither can it be denied, that the expression bears a reference to some kind of humiliation on the part of God which had previously existed. It is this humiliation which Paul justly infers from the declaration that God had ascended. And at what time did God descend lower than when Christ emptied himself? (Ἀλλ᾽ ἑαυτὸν ἐκένωσε, , Philippians 2:7.)

If ever there was a time when, after appearing to lay aside the brightness of his power, God ascended gloriously, it was when Christ was raised from our lowest condition on earth, and received into heavenly glory.

Besides, it is not necessary to inquire very carefully into the literal exposition of the Psalm, since Paul merely alludes to the prophet's words, in the same manner as, on another occasion, he accommodates to his own subject a passage taken from the writings of Moses. "The righteousness which is of faith speaketh in this manner, Say not in thine heart, who shall ascend into heaven? (that is, to bring Christ down from above;) or, who shall descend into the deep (that is, to bring up Christ again from the dead.") (Romans 10:6, Deuteronomy 30:12.) But the appropriateness of the application which Paul makes of the passage to the person of Christ is not the only ground on which it must be defended. Sufficient evidence is afforded by the Psalm itself, that this ascription of praise relates to Christ's kingdom. Not to mention other reasons which might be urged, it contains a distinct prophecy of the calling of the Gentiles.

Into the lower parts of the earth. (140) These words mean nothing more than the condition of the present life. To torture them so as to make them mean purgatory or hell, is exceedingly foolish. The argument taken from the comparative degree, "the lower parts," is quite untenable. A comparison is drawn, not between one part of the earth and another, but between the whole earth and heaven; as if he had said, that from that lofty habitation Christ descended into our deep gulf.

Verse 10

That ascended up far above all heavens; that is, beyond this created world. When Christ is said to be in heaven, we must not view him as dwelling among the spheres and numbering the stars. Heaven denotes a place higher than all the spheres, which was assigned to the Son of God after his resurrection. (141) Not that it is literally a place beyond the world, but we cannot speak of the kingdom of God without using our ordinary language. Others, again, considering that the expressions, above all heavens, and ascension into heaven, are of the same import, conclude that Christ is not separated from us by distance of place. But one point they have overlooked. When Christ is placed above the heavens, or in the heavens, all that surrounds the earth — all that lies beneath the sun and stars, beneath the whole frame of the visible world — is excluded.

That he might fill all things. To fill often signifies to Finish, and it might have that meaning here; for, by his ascension into heaven, Christ entered into the possession of the authority given to him by the Father, that he might rule and govern all things. But a more beautiful view, in my opinion, will be obtained by connecting two meanings which, though apparently contradictory, are perfectly consistent. When we hear of the ascension of Christ, it instantly strikes our minds that he is removed to a great distance from us; and so he actually is, with respect to his body and human presence. But Paul reminds us, that, while he is removed from us in bodily presence, he fills all things by the power of his Spirit. Wherever the right hand of God, which embraces heaven and earth, is displayed, Christ is spiritually present by his boundless power; although, as respects his body, the saying of Peter holds true, that

"the heaven must receive him until the times of restitution of all things, which God hath spoken by the mouth of all his holy prophets since the world began." (Acts 3:21.)

By alluding to the seeming contradiction, the apostle has added not a little beauty to his language. He ascended; but it was that he, who was formerly bounded by a little space, might fill all things But did he not fill them before? In his divine nature, I own,

72

he did; but the power of his Spirit was not so exerted, nor his presence so manifested, as after he had entered into the possession of his kingdom.

"The Holy Ghost was not yet given,
because Jesus was not yet glorified." (John 7:39.)

And again,

"It is expedient for you that I go away; for, if I go not away, the Comforter will not come to you." (John 16:7.)

In a word, when he began to sit at the right hand of the Father, he began also to fill all things. (142)

Verse 11

He returns to explain the distribution of gifts, and illustrates at greater length what he had slightly hinted, that out of this variety arises unity in the church, as the various tones in music produce sweet melody. The meaning may be thus summed up. "The external ministry of the word is also commended, on account of the advantages which it yields. Certain men appointed to that office, are employed in preaching the gospel. This is the arrangement by which the Lord is pleased to govern his church, to maintain its existence, and ultimately to secure its highest perfection."

It may excite surprise, that, when the gifts of the Holy Spirit form the subject of discussion, Paul should enumerate offices instead of gifts. I reply, when men are called by God, gifts are necessarily connected with offices. God does not confer on men the mere name of Apostles or Pastors, but also endows them with gifts, without which they cannot properly discharge their office. He whom God has appointed to be an apostle does not bear an empty and useless title; for the divine command, and the ability to perform it, go together. Let us now examine the words in detail.

And he gave. The government of the church, by the preaching of the word, is first of all declared to be no human contrivance, but a most sacred ordinance of Christ. The apostles did not appoint themselves, but were chosen by Christ; and, at the present day, true pastors do not rashly thrust themselves forward by their own judgment, but are raised up by the Lord. In short, the government of the church, by the ministry of the word, is not a contrivance of men, but an appointment made by the Son of God. As his own unalterable law, it demands our assent. They who reject or despise this ministry offer insult and rebellion to Christ its Author. It is himself who gave them; for, if he does not raise them up, there will be none. Another inference is, that no man will be fit or qualified for so distinguished an office who has not been formed and moulded by the hand of Christ himself. To Christ we owe it that we have ministers of the gospel, that they abound in necessary qualifications, that they execute the trust committed to them. All, all is his gift.

Some, apostles. The different names and offices assigned to different persons take their rise from that diversity of the members which goes to form the completeness of the whole body, — every ground of emulation, and envy, and ambition, being thus removed. If every person shall display a selfish character, shall strive to outshine his neighbor, and shall disregard all concerns but his own, — or, if more eminent persons shall be the object of envy to those who occupy a lower place, — in each, and in all of these cases, gifts are not applied to their proper use. He therefore reminds them, that the gifts bestowed on individuals are intended, not to be held for their personal and separate interests, but to be employed for the benefit of the whole. Of the offices which are here enumerated, we have already spoken at considerable length, (143) and shall now say nothing more than the exposition of the passage seems to demand. Five classes of office-bearers are mentioned, though on this point, I am aware, there is a diversity of opinion; for some consider the two last to make but one office. Leaving out of view the opinions of others, I shall proceed to state my own.

I take the word apostles not in that general sense which the derivation of the term might warrant, but in its own peculiar signification, for those highly favored persons whom Christ exalted to the highest honor. Such were the twelve, to whose number Paul was afterwards added. Their office was to spread the doctrine of the gospel throughout the whole world, to plant churches, and to erect the kingdom of Christ. They had not churches of their own committed to them; but the injunction given to all of them was, to preach the gospel wherever they went.

Next to them come the Evangelists, who were closely allied in the nature of their office, but held an inferior rank. To this class belonged Timothy and others; for, while Paul mentions them along with himself in the salutations of his epistles, he does not speak of them as his companions in the apostleship, but claims this name as peculiarly his own. The services in which the Lord employed them were auxiliary to those of the apostles, to whom they were next in rank.

To these two classes the apostle adds Prophets. By this name some understand those persons who possessed the gift of predicting future events, among whom was Agabus. (Acts 11:28.) But, for my own part, as doctrine is the present subject, I would rather define the word prophets, as on a former occasion, (144) to mean distinguished interpreters of prophecies, who, by a remarkable gift of revelation, applied them to the subjects which they had occasion to handle; not excluding, however, the gift of prophecy, by which their doctrinal instruction was usually accompanied.

Pastors and Teachers are supposed by some to denote one office, because the apostle does not, as in the other parts of the verse, say, and some, pastors; and some, teachers; but , τοὺς δὲ, ποιμένας καὶ διδασκάλους, and some, pastors and teachers Chrysostom and Augustine are of this opinion; not to mention the commentaries of Ambrose, whose observations on the subject are truly childish and unworthy of himself. I partly agree with them, that Paul speaks indiscriminately of pastors and teachers as belonging to one and the same class, and that the name teacher does, to some extent, apply to all pastors. But this does not appear to me a sufficient reason why two offices, which I find to differ from each other, should be confounded. Teaching is, no doubt, the duty of all pastors; but to maintain sound doctrine requires a talent for interpreting Scripture, and a man may be a teacher who is not qualified to preach.

Pastors, in my opinion, are those who have the charge of a particular flock; though I have no objection to their receiving the name of teachers, if it be understood that there is a distinct class of teachers, who preside both in the education of pastors and in the instruction of the whole church. It may sometimes happen, that the same person is both a pastor and a teacher, but the duties to be performed are entirely different.

It deserves attention, also, that, of the five offices which are here enumerated, not more than the last two are intended to be perpetual. Apostles, Evangelists, and Prophets were bestowed on the church for a limited time only, — except in those cases where religion has fallen into decay, and evangelists are raised up in an extraordinary manner, to restore the pure doctrine which had been lost. But without Pastors and Teachers there can be no government of the church.

Papists have some reason to complain, that their primacy, of which they boast so much, is openly insulted in this passage. The subject of discussion is the unity of the church. Paul inquires into the means by which its continuance is secured, and the outward expressions by which it is promoted, and comes at length to the government of the church. If he knew a primacy which had a fixed residence, was it not his duty, for the benefit of the whole church, to exhibit one ministerial head placed over all the members, under whose government we are collected into one body? We must either charge Paul with inexcusable neglect and foolishness, in leaving out the most appropriate and powerful argument, or we must acknowledge that this primacy is at variance with the appointment of Christ. In truth, he plainly rejects it as without foundation, when he ascribes superiority to Christ alone, and represents the apostles, and all the pastors, as indeed inferior to Him, but associated on an equal level with each other. There is no passage of Scripture by which that tyrannical hierarchy, regulated by one earthly head, is more completely overturned. Paul has been followed by Cyprian, who gives a short and clear definition of what forms the only lawful monarchy in the church. There is, he says, one bishoprick, which unites the various parts into one whole. This bishoprick he claims for Christ alone, leaving the administration of it to individuals, but in a united capacity, no one being permitted to exalt himself above others.

Verse 12

For the renewing of the saints. In this version I follow Erasmus, not because I prefer his view, but to allow the reader an opportunity of comparing his version with the Vulgate and with mine, and then choosing for himself. The old translation was, (ad consummationem ,) for the completeness. The Greek word employed by Paul is καταρτισμός, which signifies literally the adaptation of things possessing symmetry and proportion; just as, in the human body, the members are united in a proper and regular manner; so that the word comes to signify perfection. But as Paul intended to express here a just and orderly arrangement, I prefer the word (constitutio) settlement or constitution, taking it in that sense in which a commonwealth, or kingdom, or province, is said to be settled, when confusion gives place to the regular administration of law.

For the work of the ministry. God might himself have performed this work, if he had chosen; but he has committed it to theministry of men. This is intended to anticipate an objection. "Cannot the church be constituted and properly arranged, without the instrumentality of men?" Paul asserts that a ministry is required, because such is the will of God.

For the edifying of the body of Christ. This is the same thing with what he had formerly denominated the settlement orperfecting of the saints. Our true completeness and perfection consist in our being united in the one body of Christ. No language more highly commendatory of the ministry of the word could have been employed, than to ascribe to it this effect. What is more excellent than to produce the true and complete perfection of the church? And yet this work, so admirable and divine, is here declared by the apostle to be accomplished by the external ministry of the word. That those who neglect this instrument should hope to become perfect in Christ is utter madness. Yet such are the fanatics, on the one hand, who pretend to be favored with secret revelations of the Spirit, — and proud men, on the other, who imagine that to them the private reading of the Scriptures is enough, and that they have no need of the ordinary ministry of the church.

If the edification of the church proceeds from Christ alone, he has surely a right to prescribe in what manner it shall be edified. But Paul expressly states, that, according to the command of Christ, no real union or perfection is attained, but by the outward preaching. We must allow ourselves to be ruled and taught by men. This is the universal rule, which extends equally to the highest and to the lowest. The church is the common mother of all the godly, which bears, nourishes, and brings up children to God, kings and peasants alike; and this is done by the ministry. Those who neglect or despise this order choose to be wiser than Christ. Woe to the pride of such men! It is, no doubt, a thing in itself possible that divine influence alone should make us perfect without human assistance. But the present inquiry is not what the power of God can accomplish, but what is the will of God and the appointment of Christ. In employing human instruments for accomplishing their salvation, God has conferred on men no ordinary favor. Nor can any exercise be found better adapted to promote unity than to gather around the common doctrine — the standard of our General.

Verse 13

Till we all come. Paul had already said, that by the ministry of men the church is regulated and governed, so as to attain the highest perfection. But his commendation of the ministry is now carried farther. The necessity for which he had pleaded is not confined to a single day, but continues to the end. Or, to speak more plainly, he reminds his readers that the use of the ministry is not temporal, like that of a school for children, (παιδαγωγία, , Galatians 3:24,) but constant, so long as we remain in the world. Enthusiasts dream that the use of the ministry ceases as soon as we have been led to Christ. Proud men, who carry their desire of knowledge beyond what is proper, look down with contempt on the elementary instruction of childhood. But Paul maintains that we must persevere in this course till all our deficiencies are supplied; that we must make progress till death, under the teaching of Christ alone; and that we must not be ashamed to be the scholars of the church, to which Christ has committed our education.

In the unity of the faith. But ought not the unity of the faith to reign among us from the very commencement? It does reign, I acknowledge, among the sons of God, but not so perfectly as to make them come together. Such is the weakness of our nature, that it is enough if every day brings some nearer to others, and all nearer to Christ. The expression, coming together, denotes that closest union to which we still aspire, and which we shall never reach, until this garment of the flesh, which is always accompanied by some remains of ignorance and weakness, shall have been laid aside.

And of the knowledge of the Son of God. This clause appears to be added for the sake of explanation. It was the apostle's intention to explain what is the nature of true faith, and in what it consists; that is, when the Son of God is known. To the Son of God alone faith ought to look; on him it relies; in him it rests and terminates. If it proceed farther, it will disappear, and will no longer be faith, but a delusion. Let us remember, that true faith confines its view so entirely to Christ, that it neither knows, nor desires to know, anything else.

Into a perfect man. This must be read in immediate connection with what goes before; as if he had said, "What is the highest perfection of Christians? How is that perfection attained?" Full manhood is found in Christ; for foolish men do not, in a proper manner, seek their perfection in Christ. It ought to be held as a fixed principle among us, that all that is out of Christ is hurtful and destructive. Whoever is a man in Christ, is, in every respect, a perfect man.

The AGE of fullness means — full or mature age. No mention is made of old age, for in the Christian progress no place for it is found. Whatever becomes old has a tendency to decay; but the vigor of this spiritual life is continually advancing.

Verse 14

That we may be no more children. Having spoken of that perfect manhood, towards which we are proceeding throughout the whole course of our life, he reminds us that, during such a progress, we ought not to resemble children. An intervening period is thus pointed out between childhood and man's estate. Those are "children" who have not yet advanced a step in the way of the Lord, but who still hesitate, — who have not yet determined what road they ought to choose, but move sometimes in one direction and sometimes in another, always doubtful, always wavering. Those, again, who are thoroughly founded in the doctrine of Christ, though not yet perfect, have so much wisdom and vigor as to choose properly, and proceed steadily, in the right course. Thus we find that the life of believers, marked by a constant desire and progress towards those attainments which they shall ultimately reach, bears a resemblance to youth. At no period of this life are we men. But let not such a statement be carried to the other extreme, as if there were no progress beyond childhood. After being born to Christ, we ought to grow, so as "not to be children in understanding." (1 Corinthians 14:20.) Hence it appears what kind of Christianity the Popish system must be, when the pastors labor, to the utmost of their power, to keep the people in absolute infancy.

78

Tossed to and fro, and carried about. The distressing hesitation of those who do not place absolute reliance on the word of the Lord, is illustrated by two striking metaphors. The first is taken from small ships, exposed to the fury of the billows in the open sea, holding no fixed course, guided neither by skill nor design, but hurried along by the violence of the tempest. The next is taken from straws, or other light substances, which are carried hither and thither as the wind drives them, and often in opposite directions. Such must be the changeable and unsteady character of all who do not rest on the foundation of God's eternal truth. It is their just punishment for looking, not to God, but to men. Paul declares, on the other hand, that faith, which rests on the word of God, stands unshaken against all the attacks of Satan.

By every wind of doctrine. By a beautiful metaphor, all the doctrines of men, by which we are drawn away from the simplicity of the gospel, are called winds God gave us his word, by which we might have placed ourselves beyond the possibility of being moved; but, giving way to the contrivances of men, we are carried about in all directions.

By the cunning of men. There will always be impostors, who make insidious attacks upon our faith; but, if we are fortified by the truth of God, their efforts will be unavailing. Both parts of this statement deserve our careful attention. When new sects, or wicked tenets, spring up, many persons become alarmed. But the attempts of Satan to darken, by his falsehoods, the pure doctrine of Christ, are at no time interrupted; and it is the will of God that these struggles should be the trial of our faith. When we are informed, on the other hand, that the best and readiest defense against every kind of error is to bring forward that doctrine which we have learned from Christ and his apostles, this surely is no ordinary consolation.

With what awful wickedness, then, are Papists chargeable, who take away from the word of God everything like certainty, and maintain that there is no steadiness of faith, but what depends on the authority of men! If a man entertain any doubt, it is in vain to bid him consult the word of God: he must abide by their decrees. But we have embraced the law, the prophets, and the gospel. Let us therefore confidently expect that we shall reap the advantage which is here promised, — that all the impostures of men will do us no harm. They will attack us, indeed, but they will not prevail. We are entitled, I acknowledge, to look for the dispensation of sound doctrine from the church, for God has committed it to her charge; but when Papists avail themselves of the disguise of the church for burying doctrine, they give sufficient proof that they have a diabolical synagogue.

The Greek word κυβεία, which I have translated cunning, is taken from players at dice, who are accustomed to practice many arts of deception. The words , ἐν πανουργίᾳ, by craftiness, intimate that the ministers of Satan are deeply skilled in imposture; and it is added, that they keep watch, in order to insnare, (πρὸς τὴν μεθοδείαν τῶς πλάνης.) All this should rouse and sharpen our minds to profit by the word of God. If we neglect to do so, we may fall into the snares of our enemies, and endure the severe punishment of our sloth.

Verse 15

But, speaking the truth. Having already said that we ought not to be children, destitute of reason and judgment, he now enjoins us to grow up in the truth. (145) Though we have not arrived at man's estate, we ought at least, as we have already said, to be advanced children. The truth of God ought to have such a firm hold of us, that all the contrivances and attacks of Satan shall not draw us from our course; and yet, as we have not hitherto attained full and complete strength, we must make progress until death.

He points out the design of this progress, that Christ may be the head, "that in all things he may have the pre-eminence," (Colossians 1:18,) and that in him alone we may grow in vigor or in stature. Again, we see that no man is excepted; all are enjoined to be subject, and to take their own places in the body.

What aspect then does Popery present, but that of a crooked, deformed person? Is not the whole symmetry of the church destroyed, when one man, acting in opposition to the head, refuses to be reckoned one of the members? The Papists deny this, and allege that the Pope is nothing more than a ministerial head. But such cavils do them no service. The tyranny of their idol must be acknowledged to be altogether inconsistent with that order which Paul here recommends. In a word, a healthful condition of the church requires that Christ alone "must increase," and all others "must decrease." (John 3:30.) Whatever increase we obtain must be regulated in such a manner, that we shall remain in our own place, and contribute to exalt the head.

When he bids us give heed to the truth in love, he uses the preposition in, (ἐν,) like the corresponding Hebrew preposition ב, (beth,) as signifying with, — speaking the truth With love (146) If each individual, instead of attending exclusively to his own concerns, shall desire mutual intercourse, there will be agreeable and general progress. Such, the Apostle assures us, must be the nature of this harmony, that men shall not be suffered to forget the claims of truth, or, disregarding them, to frame an agreement according to their own views. This proves the wickedness of the

80

Papists, who lay aside the word of God, and labor to force our compliance with their decisions.

Verse 16

From whom the whole body. All our increase should tend to exalt more highly the glory of Christ. This is now proved by the best possible reason. It is he who supplies all our wants, and without whose protection we cannot be safe. As the root conveys sap to the whole tree, so all the vigor which we possess must flow to us from Christ. There are three things here which deserve our attention. The first is what has now been stated. All the life or health which is diffused through the members flows from the head; so that the members occupy a subordinate rank. The second is, that, by the distribution made, the limited share of each renders the communication between all the members absolutely necessary. The third is, that, without mutual love, the health of the body cannot be maintained. Through the members, as canals, is conveyed from the head all that is necessary for the nourishment of the body. While this connection is upheld, the body is alive and healthy. Each member, too, has its own proper share, — according to the effectual working in the measure of every part.

Lastly, he shows that by love the church is edified, — to the edifying of itself in love. This means that no increase is advantageous, which does not bear a just proportion to the whole body. That man is mistaken who desires his own separate growth. If a leg or arm should grow to a prodigious size, or the mouth be more fully distended, would the undue enlargement of those parts be otherwise than injurious to the whole frame? In like manner, if we wish to be considered members of Christ, let no man be anything for himself, but let us all be whatever we are for the benefit of each other. This is accomplished by love; and where it does not reign, there is no "edification," but an absolute scattering of the church.

Verse 17

This I say therefore. That government which Christ has appointed for the edification of his church has now been considered. He next inquires what fruits the doctrine of the gospel ought to yield in the lives of Christians; or, if you prefer it, he begins to explain minutely the nature of that edification by which doctrine ought to be followed.

That ye henceforth walk not in vanity. He first exhorts them to renounce the vanity of unbelievers, arguing from its inconsistency with their present views. That those who have been taught in the school of Christ, and enlightened by the doctrine of salvation, should follow vanity, and in no respect differ from those unbelieving and blind nations on whom no light of truth has ever shone, would be singularly foolish. On this ground he very properly calls upon them to demonstrate, by their life, that they had gained some advantage by becoming the disciples of Christ. To impart to his exhortation the greater earnestness, he beseeches them by the name of God, — this I say and testify in the Lord, (147) — reminding them, that, if they despised this instruction, they must one day give an account.

As other Gentiles walk. He means those who had not yet been converted to Christ. But, at the same time, he reminds the Ephesians how necessary it was that they should repent, since by nature they resembled lost and condemned men. The miserable and shocking condition of other nations is held out as the motive to a change of disposition. He asserts that believers differ from unbelievers; and points out, as we shall see, the causes of this difference. With regard to the former, he accuses their mind of vanity: and let us remember, that he speaks generally of all who have not been renewed by the Spirit of Christ.

In the vanity of their mind. Now, the mind holds the highest rank in the human constitution, is the seat of reason, presides over the will, and restrains sinful desires; so that our theologians of the Sorbonne are in the habit of calling her the Queen. But, Paul makes the mind to consist of nothing else than vanity; and, as if he had not expressed his meaning strongly enough, he gives no better title to her daughter, the understanding. Such is my interpretation of the word διανοία; for, though it signifies the thought, yet, as it is in the singular number, it refers to the thinking faculty. Plato, about the close of his Sixth Book on a Republic, assigns to διανοία an intermediate place between νόησις and πίστις but his observations are so entirely confined to geometrical subjects, as not to admit of application to this passage. Having formerly asserted that men see nothing, Paul now adds, that they are blind in reasoning, even on the most important subjects.

Let men now go and be proud of free-will, whose guidance is here marked by so deep disgrace. But experience, we shall be told, is openly at variance with this opinion; for men are not so blind as to be incapable of seeing anything, nor so vain as to be incapable of forming any judgment. I answer, with respect to the kingdom of God, and all that relates to the spiritual life, the light of human reason differs little from darkness; for, before it has pointed out the road, it is extinguished; and its power of perception is little else than blindness, for ere it has reached the fruit, it is gone. The true principles held by the human mind resemble sparks; (148) but these are choked by the depravity of our nature, before they have been applied to their proper use. All men know, for instance, that there is a God, and that it is our duty to worship him; but such is the power of sin and ignorance, that from this confused knowledge we pass all at once to an idol, and worship it in the place of God. And even in the worship of God, it leads to great errors, particularly in the first table of the law.

As to the second objection, our judgment does indeed agree with the law of God in regard to the mere outward actions; but sinful desire, which is the source of everything evil, escapes our notice. Besides, Paul does not speak merely of the natural blindness which we brought with us from the womb, but refers also to a still grosser blindness, by which, as we shall afterwards see, God punishes former transgressions. We conclude with observing, that the reason and understanding which men naturally possess, make them in the sight of God without excuse; but, so long as they allow themselves to live according to their natural disposition, they can only wander, and fall, and stumble in their purposes and actions. Hence it appears in what estimation and value false worship must appear in the sight of God, when it proceeds from the gulf of vanity and the maze of ignorance.

Verse 18

Being alienated from the life of God. The life of God may either mean what is accounted life in the sight of God, as in that passage,

"they loved the praise of men more than the praise of God, "
(John 12:43,)

or, that life which God bestows on his elect by the Spirit of regeneration. In both cases the meaning is the same. Our ordinary life, as men, is nothing more than an empty image of life, not only because it quickly passes, but also because, while we live, our souls, not keeping close to God, are dead. There are three kinds of life in this world. The first is animal life, which consists only of motion and the bodily senses, and which we have in common with the brutes; the second is human life, which we have as the children of Adam; and the third is that supernatural life, which believers alone obtain. And all of them are from God, so that each of them may be called the life of God. As to the first, Paul, in his sermon at Athens, says, (Acts 17:28,) "In him we live, and move, and have our being;" and the Psalmist says,

"Send forth thy Spirit, and they shall be created; and thou wilt renew the face of the earth." (Psalms 104:30.)

Of the second Job says,

"Thou hast granted me life, and thy visitation hath preserved my spirit." (Job 10:12.)

But the regeneration of believers is here called, by way of eminence, the life of God, because then does God truly live in us, and we enjoy his life, when he governs us by his Spirit. Of this life all men who are not new creatures in Christ are declared by Paul to be destitute. So long, then, as we remain in the flesh, that is, in ourselves, how wretched must be our condition! We may now form a judgment of all the moral virtues, as they are called; for what sort of actions will that life produce which, Paul affirms, is not the life of God? Before anything good can begin to proceed from us, we must first be renewed by the grace of Christ. This will be the commencement of a true, and, as the phrase is, a vital life.

On account of the ignorance that is in them. We ought to attend to the reason which is here assigned; for, as the knowledge of God is the true life of the soul, so, on the contrary, ignorance is the death of it. And lest we should adopt the opinion of philosophers, that ignorance, which leads us into mistakes, is only an incidental evil, Paul shews that it has its root in the blindness of their heart, by which he intimates that it dwells in their very nature. The first blindness, therefore, which covers the minds of men, is the punishment of original sin; because Adam, after his revolt, was deprived of the true light of God, in the absence of which there is nothing but fearful darkness.

Verse 19

Who being past feeling. The account which had been given of natural depravity is followed by a description of the worst of all evils, brought upon men by their own sinful conduct. Having destroyed the sensibilities of the heart, and allayed the stings of remorse, they abandon themselves to all manner of iniquity. We are by nature corrupt and prone to evil; nay, we are wholly inclined to evil. Those who are destitute of the Spirit of Christ give loose reins to self-indulgence, till fresh offenses, producing others in constant succession, bring down upon them the wrath of God. The voice of God, proclaimed by an accusing conscience, still continues to be heard; but, instead of producing its proper effects, appears rather to harden them against all admonition. On account of such obstinacy, they deserve to be altogether forsaken by God.

The usual symptom of their having been thus forsaken is — the insensibility to pain, which is here described — being past feeling. Unmoved by the approaching judgment of God, whom they offend, they go on at their ease, and fearlessly indulge without restraint in the pleasures of sin. No shame is felt, no regard to character is maintained. The gnawing of a guilty conscience, tormented by the dread of the Divine judgment, may be compared to the porch of hell; but such hardened security as this — is a whirlpool which swallows up and destroys. As Solomon says,

"When the wicked is come to the deep, he despiseth it."
(Proverbs 18:3.)

Most properly, therefore, does Paul exhibit that dreadful example of Divine vengeance, in which men forsaken by God — having laid conscience to sleep, and destroyed all fear of the Divine judgment, — in a word, being past feeling, — surrender themselves with brutal violence to all wickedness. This is not universally the case. Many even of the reprobate are restrained by God, whose infinite goodness prevents the absolute confusion in which the world would otherwise be involved. The consequence is, that such open lust, such unrestrained intemperance, does not appear in all. It is enough that the lives of some present such a mirror, fitted to awaken our alarm lest anything similar should happen to ourselves.

Lasciviousness (ἀσελγεία) appears to me to denote that wantonness with which the flesh indulges in intemperance and licentiousness, when not restrained by the Spirit of God. Uncleanness is put for scandalous enormities of every description. It is added, with greediness. The Greek word πλεονεξία, which is so translated, often signifies covetousness, (Luke 12:15; 2 Peter 2:14,) and is so explained by some in this passage; but I cannot adopt that view. Depraved and wicked desires being insatiable, Paul represents them as attended and followed by greediness, which is the contrary of moderation.

Verse 20

But ye have not. He now draws a contrast of a Christian life, so as to make it evident how utterly inconsistent it is with the character of a godly man to defile himself regardlessly with the abominations of the Gentiles. Because the Gentiles walk in darkness, therefore they do not distinguish between right and wrong; but those on whom the truth of God shines ought to live in a different manner. That those to whom the vanity of the senses is a rule of life, should yield themselves up to base lusts, is not surprising; but the doctrine of Christ teaches us to renounce our natural dispositions. He whose life differs not from that of unbelievers, has learned nothing of Christ; for the knowledge of Christ cannot be separated from the mortification of the flesh.

Verse 21

If ye have heard him. To excite their attention and earnestness the more, he not only tells them that they had heard Christ, but employs a still stronger expression, ye have been taught in him, as if he had said, that this doctrine had not been slightly pointed out, but faithfully delivered and explained.

As the truth is in Jesus. This contains a reproof of that superficial knowledge of the gospel, by which many are elated, who are wholly unacquainted with newness of life. They think that they are exceedingly wise, but the apostle pronounces it to be a false and mistaken opinion. There is a twofold knowledge of Christ, — one, which is true and genuine, — and another, which is counterfeit and spurious. Not that, strictly speaking, there are two kinds; but most men falsely imagine that they know Christ, while they know nothing but what is carnal. In another Epistle he says,

"If any man be in Christ, let him be a new creature."
(2 Corinthians 5:17.)

So here he affirms that any knowledge of Christ, which is not accompanied by mortification of the flesh, is not true and sincere.

Verse 22

That ye put off. He demands from a Christian man repentance, or a new life, which he makes to consist of self-denial and the regeneration of the Holy Spirit. Beginning with the first, he enjoins us to lay aside, or put off the old man, employing the metaphor of garments, which we have already had occasion to explain. The old man, — as we have repeatedly stated, in expounding the sixth chapter of the Epistle to the Romans, and other passages where it occurs, — means the natural disposition which we bring with us from our mother's womb. In two persons, Adam and Christ, he describes to us what may be called two natures. As we are first born of Adam, the depravity of nature which we derive from him is called the Old man; and as we are born again in Christ, the amendment of this sinful nature is called the New man. In a word, he who desires to put off the old man must renounce his nature. To suppose that the words Old andNew contain an allusion to the Old and New Testaments, is exceedingly unphilosophical.

Concerning the former conversation. To make it more evident that this exhortation to the Ephesians was not unnecessary, he reminds them of their former life. "Before Christ revealed himself to your minds, the old man reigned in you; and therefore, if you desire to lay him aside, you must renounce your former life." Which is corrupted. He describes the old man from the fruits, that is, from the wicked desires, which allure men to destruction; for the word, corrupt, alludes to old age, which is closely allied to corruption. Let us beware of considering the deceitful lusts, as the Papists do, to mean nothing more than the gross and visible lusts, which are generally acknowledged to be base. The word includes also those dispositions which, instead of being censured, are sometimes applauded, — such as ambition, cunning, and everything that proceeds either from self-love or from want of confidence in God.

Verse 23

And be renewed. The second part of the rule for a devout and holy life is to live, not in our own spirit, but in the Spirit of Christ. But what is meant by — the spirit of your mind? I understand it simply to mean, — Be renewed, not only with respect to the inferior appetites or desires, which are manifestly sinful, but with respect also to that part of the soul which is reckoned most noble and excellent. And here again, he brings forward to view that Queen which philosophers are accustomed almost to adore. There is an implied contrast between the spirit of our mind and the Divine and heavenly Spirit, who produces in us another and a new mind. How much there is in us that is sound or uncorrupted may be easily gathered from this passage, which enjoins us to correct chiefly the reason or mind, in which we are apt to imagine that there is nothing but what is virtuous and deserves commendation.

Verse 24

And that ye put on the new man. All that is meant is, "Be renewed in the spirit, or, be renewed within or completely, — beginning with the mind, which appears to be the part most free from all taint of sin." What is added about the creation, may refer either to the first creation of man, or to the second creation, which is effected by the grace of Christ. Both expositions will be true. Adam was at first created after the image of God, and reflected, as in a mirror, the Divine righteousness; but that image, having been defaced by sin, must now be restored in Christ. The regeneration of the godly is indeed — as we have formerly explained (149) — nothing else than the formation anew of the image of God in them. There is, no doubt, a far more rich and powerful manifestation of Divine grace in this second creation than in the first; but our highest perfection is uniformly represented in Scripture as consisting in our conformity and resemblance to God. Adam lost the image which he had originally received, and therefore it becomes necessary that it shall be restored to us by Christ. The design contemplated by regeneration is to recall us from our wanderings to that end for which we were created.

In righteousness. If righteousness be taken as a general term for uprightness, holiness will be something higher, or that purity which lies in being devoted to the service of God. I am rather inclined to consider holiness as referring to the first table, and righteousness to the second table, of the law, as in the song of Zacharias,

"That we may serve him in holiness and righteousness, all the days of our life." (Luke 1:74.)

Plato lays down the distinction correctly, that holiness (ὁσιότης) lies in the worship of God, and that the other part,righteousness, (δικαιοσύνη,) bears a reference to men. The genitive, of truth, (τῶς αληθείας,) is put in the place of an adjective, and refers to both terms; so that, while it literally runs, in righteousness and holiness of truth, the meaning is, in true righteousness and holiness. He warns us that both ought to be sincere; because we have to do with God, whom it is impossible to deceive.

Verse 25

Wherefore, putting away lying. From this head of doctrine, that is, from the righteousness of the new man, all godly exhortations flow, like streams from a fountain; for if all the precepts which relate to life were collected, yet, without this principle, they would be of little value. Philosophers take a different method; but, in the doctrine of godliness, there is no other way than this for regulating the life. Now, therefore, he comes to lay down particular exhortations, drawn from the general doctrine. Having concluded from the truth of the gospel, that righteousness and holiness ought to be true, he now argues from the general statement to a particular instance, that every man should speak truth with his neighbour. Lying is here put for every kind of deceit, hypocrisy, or cunning; and truth for honest dealing. He demands that every kind of communication between them shall be sincere; and enforces it by this consideration, for we are members one of another. That members should not agree among themselves, — that they should act in a deceitful manner towards each other, is prodigious wickedness.

Verse 26

Be ye angry, and sin not. Whether or not the apostle had in his eye a part of the fourth Psalm is uncertain. The words used by him (Ὀργίζεσθε καὶ υἡ ἁμαρτάνετε) occur in the Greek translation, though the word ὀργίζεσθε, which is translated, be ye angry, is considered by some to mean tremble. (150) The Hebrew verb רגז (ragaz) signifies either to be agitated by anger, or, to tremble. As to the passage of the Psalm, the idea of trembling will be quite appropriate. "Do not choose to resemble madmen, who rush fearlessly in any direction, but let the dread of being accounted foolhardy keep you in awe." The word sometimes signifies to strive or quarrel, as, in that instance, (Genesis 45:24,) "See that ye fall not out by the way;" and accordingly, the Psalmist adds, "Commune with your own heart, and be still," — abstain from furious encounters.

In my opinion, Paul merely alludes to the passage with the following view. There are three faults by which we offend God in being angry. The first is, when our anger arises from slight causes, and often from no cause whatever, or at least from private injuries or offenses. The second is, when we go beyond the proper bounds, and are hurried into intemperate excesses. The third is, when our anger, which ought to have been directed against ourselves or against sins, is turned against our brethren. Most appropriately, therefore, did Paul, when he wished to describe the proper limitation of anger, employ the well-known passage, Be ye angry, and sin not. We comply with this injunction, if the objects of our anger are sought, not in others, but in ourselves, — if we pour out our indignation against our own faults. With respect to others, we ought to be angry, not at their persons, but at their faults; nor ought we to be excited to anger by private offenses, but by zeal for the glory of the Lord. Lastly, our anger, after a reasonable time, ought to be allowed to subside, without mixing itself with the violence of carnal passions.

Let not the sun go down. It is scarcely possible, however, but that we shall sometimes give way to improper and sinful passion, — so strong is the tendency of the human mind to what is evil. Paul therefore suggests a second remedy, that we shall quickly suppress our anger, and not suffer it to gather strength by continuance. The first remedy was, Be ye angry, and sin not; but, as the great weakness of human nature renders this exceedingly difficult, the next is — not to cherish wrath too long in our minds, or allow it sufficient time to become strong. He enjoins accordingly, let not the sun go down upon your wrath. If at any time we happen to be angry, let us endeavor to be appeased before the sun has set.

Verse 27

Neither give place (τῷ διαβόλῳ) to the devil. I am aware of the interpretation which some give of this passage. Erasmus, who translates it, "neither give place to the Slanderer," (calumniatori ,) shews plainly that he understood it as referring to malicious men. But I have no doubt, Paul's intention was, to guard us against allowing Satan to take possession of our minds, and, by keeping in his hands this citadel, to do whatever he pleases. We feel every day how impossible, or, at least, how difficult it is to cure long-continued hatred. What is the cause of this, but that, instead of resisting the devil, we yield up to him the possession of our heart? Before the poison of hatred has found its way into the heart, anger must be thoroughly dislodged.

Verse 28

Let him that stole steal no more. This includes not merely the grosser thefts which are punished by human laws, but those of a more concealed nature, which do not fall under the cognizance of men, — every kind of depredation by which we seize the property of others. But he does not simply forbid us to take that property in an unjust or unlawful manner. He enjoins us to assist our brethren, as far as lies in our power.

That he may have to give to him that needeth. "Thou who formerly stolest must not only obtain thy subsistence by lawful and harmless toil, but must give assistance to others." He is first required to labor, working with his hands, that he may not supply his wants at the expense of his brethren, but may support life by honorable labor. But the love which we owe to our neighbor carries us much farther. No one must live to himself alone, and neglect others. All must labor to supply each other's necessities.

But a question arises, does Paul oblige all men to labor with their hands? This would be excessively hard. I reply, the meaning is plain, if it be duly considered. Every man is forbidden to steal. But many people are in the habit of pleading want, and that excuse is obviated by enjoining themrather to labor (μᾶλλον δε κοπιάτω) with their hands. As if he had said, "No condition, however hard or disagreeable, can entitle any man to do injury to another, or even to refrain from contributing to the necessities of his brethren.

The thing which is good. This latter clause, which contains an argument from the greater to the less, gives no small additional strength to the exhortation. As there are many occupations which do little to promote the lawful enjoyments of men, he recommends to them to choose those employments which yield the greatest advantage to their neighbors. We need not wonder at this. If those trades which can have no other effect than to lead men into immorality, were denounced by heathens — and Cicero among the number — as highly disgraceful, would an apostle of Christ reckon them among the lawful callings of God?

Verse 29

No filthy speech. He first forbids believers to use any filthy language, including under this name all those expressions which are wont to be employed for the purpose of inflaming lust. Not satisfied with the removal of the vice, he enjoins them to frame their discourse for edification. In another Epistle he says, "Let your speech be seasoned with salt." (Colossians 4:6.) Here a different phrase is employed, if any (speech) be good to the use of edifying, which means simply, if it be useful. The genitive, of use, may no doubt be viewed, according to the Hebrew idiom, as put for an adjective, so that for the edification of use (πρὸς οἰκοδομὴν τῶς χρείας) may mean for useful edification; but when I consider how frequently, and in how extensive a meaning, the metaphor of edifying occurs in Paul's writings, I prefer the former exposition. The edification of use will thus mean the progress of our edification, for to edify is to carry forward. To explain the manner in which this is done, he adds, that it may impart grace to the hearers, meaning by the word grace, comfort, advice, and everything that aids the salvation of the soul.

Verse 30

And grieve not. As the Holy Spirit dwells in us, to him every part of our soul and of our body ought to be devoted. But if we give ourselves up to aught that is impure, we may be said to drive him away from making his abode with us; and, to express this still more familiarly, human affections, such as joy and grief, are ascribed to the Holy Spirit. (151) Endeavour that the Holy Spirit may dwell cheerfully with you, as in a pleasant and joyful dwelling, and give him no occasion for grief. Some take a different view of it, that we grieve the Holy Spirit in others, when we offend by filthy language, or, in any other way, godly brethren, who are led by the Spirit of God. (Romans 8:14.) Whatever is contrary to godliness is not only disrelished by godly ears, but is no sooner heard than it produces in them deep grief and pain. But that Paul's meaning was different appears from what follows.

By whom ye are sealed. As God has sealed us by his Spirit, we grieve him when we do not follow his guidance, but pollute ourselves by wicked passions. No language can adequately express this solemn truth, that the Holy Spirit rejoices and is glad on our account, when we are obedient to him in all things, and neither think nor speak anything, but what is pure and holy; and, on the other hand, is grieved, when we admit anything into our minds that is unworthy of our calling. Now, let any man reflect what shocking wickedness there must be in grieving the Holy Spirit to such a degree as to compel him to withdraw from us. The same mode of speaking is used by the prophet Isaiah, but in a different sense; for he merely says, that they "vexed his Holy Spirit," (Isaiah 63:10.) in the same sense in which we are accustomed to speak of vexing the mind of a man. By whom ye are sealed. The Spirit of God is the seal, by which we are distinguished from the wicked, and which is impressed on our hearts as a sure evidence of adoption.

Unto the day of redemption, — that is, till God conduct us into the possession of the promised inheritance. That day is usually called the day of redemption, because we shall then be at length delivered out of all our afflictions. It is unnecessary to make any observations on this phrase, in addition to what have already been made in expounding Romans 8:23, and 1 Corinthians 1:30. In this passage, the word sealed may have a different meaning from that which it usually bears, — that God has impressed his Spirit as his mark upon us, that he may recognize as his children those whom he perceives to bear that mark.

Verse 31

Let all bitterness. He again condemns anger; but, on the present occasion, views in connection with it those offenses by which it is usually accompanied, such as noisy disputes and reproaches. Between wrath and anger (Θυμὸν καὶ ὀργὴν) there is little difference, except that the former denotes the power, and the latter the act; but here, the only difference is, that anger is a more sudden attack. The correction of all the rest will be greatly aided by the removal of malice. By this term he expresses that depravity of mind which is opposed to humanity and justice, and which is usually called malignity.

Verse 32

And be ye kind one to another. With bitterness he contrasts kindness, or gentleness of countenance, language, and manners. And as this virtue will never reign in us, unless attended by compassion, (ουμπάθεια,) he recommends to us to be tender-hearted This will lead us not only to sympathize with the distresses of our brethren, as if they were our own, but to cultivate that true humanity which is affected by everything that happens to them, in the same manner as if we were in their situation. The contrary of this is the cruelty of those iron-hearted, barbarous men, by whom the sufferings of others are beheld without any concern whatever.

Forgiving one another. The Greek word here renderedforgiving, (χαριζόμενοι ἑαυτοῖς,) is supposed by to mean beneficence. Erasmus, accordingly, renders it (largientes) bountiful. Though the word admits of that meaning, yet the context induces me to prefer the other view, that we should be ready to forgive It may sometimes happen, that men are kind and tender-hearted, and yet, when they receive improper treatment, do not so easily forgive injuries. That those whose kindness of heart in other respects disposes them to acts of humanity, may not fail in their duty through the ingratitude of men, he exhorts them to discover a readiness to lay aside resentment. To give his exhortation the greater weight, he holds out the example of God, who has forgiven to us, through Christ, far more than any mortal man can forgive to his brethren. (152)

Verse 1

Be ye therefore followers. The same principle is followed out and enforced by the consideration that children ought to be like their father. He reminds us that we are the children of God, and that therefore we ought, as far as possible, to resemble Him in acts of kindness. It is impossible not to perceive, that the division of chapters, in the present instance, is particularly unhappy, as it has made a separation between parts of the subject which are very closely related. If, then, we are the children of God, we ought to be followers of God. Christ also declares, that, unless we shew kindness to the unworthy, we cannot be the children of our heavenly Father.

"Love your enemies, bless them that curse you, do good to them that hate you, and pray for them who despitefully use you and persecute you; that ye may be the children of your Father which is in heaven; for he maketh his sun to rise on the evil and on the good, and sendeth rain on the just and on the unjust."
(Matthew 5:44.) (153)

Verse 2

And walk in love as Christ also hath loved us. Having called on us to imitate God, he now calls on us to imitate Christ, who is our true model. We ought to embrace each other with that love with which Christ has embraced us, for what we perceive in Christ is our true guide.

And gave himself for us. This was a remarkable proof of the highest love. Forgetful, as it were, of himself, Christ spared not his own life, that he might redeem us from death. If we desire to be partakers of this benefit, we must cultivate similar affections toward our neighbors. Not that any of us has reached such high perfection, but all must aim and strive according to the measure of their ability.

An offering and a sacrifice to God of a sweet smelling savor. While this statement leads us to admire the grace of Christ, it bears directly on the present subject. No language, indeed, can fully represent the consequences and efficacy of Christ's death. This is the only price by which we are reconciled to God. The doctrine of faith on this subject holds the highest rank. But the more extraordinary the discoveries which have reached us of the Redeemer's kindness, the more strongly are we bound to his service. Besides, we may infer from Paul's words, that, unless we love one another, none of our duties will be acceptable in the sight of God. If the reconciliation of men, effected by Christ, was a sacrifice of a sweet smelling savor, (154) we, too, shall be "unto God a sweet savor," (2 Corinthians 2:15,) when this holy perfume is spread over us. To this applies the saying of Christ,

"Leave thy gift before the altar, and go and be reconciled to thy brother." (Matthew 5:24.)

Verse 3

But fornication. This chapter, and the Colossians 3:0, contain many parallel passages, which an intelligent reader will be at no loss to compare without my assistance. Three things are here enumerated, which the apostle desires Christians to hold in such abhorrence, that they shall not even be named, or, in other words, shall be entirely unknown among them. By uncleanness he means all base and impure lusts; so that this word differs from fornication, only as the whole class differs from a single department. The third is covetousness, which is nothing more than an immoderate desire of gain. To this precept he adds the authoritative declaration, that he demands nothing from them but that which becometh saints, — manifestly excluding from the number and fellowship of the saints all fornicators, and impure and covetous persons.

Verse 4

Neither filthiness. To those three — other three are now added. By filthiness I understand all that is indecent or inconsistent with the modesty of the godly. By foolish talking I understand conversations that are either unprofitably or wickedly foolish; and as it frequently happens that idle talk is concealed under the garb of jesting or wit, he expressly mentions pleasantry, — which is so agreeable as to seem worthy of commendation, — and condemns it as a part of foolish talking The Greek word εὐτραπελία is often used by heathen writers, in a good sense, for that ready and ingenious pleasantry in which able and intelligent men may properly indulge. But as it is exceedingly difficult to be witty without becoming satirical, and as jesting itself carries in it a portion of conceit not at all in keeping with the character of a godly man, Paul very properly dissuades from this practice. (155) Of all the three offenses now mentioned, Paul declares that they are not convenient, or, in other words, that they are inconsistent with Christian duty.

But rather grace. Others render it giving of thanks; but I prefer Jerome's interpretation. With the vices which had been formerly mentioned it was proper that Paul should contrast something of a general character, displaying itself in all our communications with each other. If he had said, "While they take pleasure in idle or abusive talk, do you give thanks to God," the exhortation would have been too

96

limited. The Greek word , εὐχαριστία, though it usually signifies Thanksgiving, admits of being translated Grace. "All our conversations ought to be, in the true sense of the words, sweet and graceful; and this end will be gained if the useful and the agreeable are properly mingled."

Verse 5

For this ye know. If his readers were at all captivated by the allurements of those vices which have been enumerated, the consequence would be that they would lend a hesitating or careless ear to his admonitions. He determines, therefore, to alarm them by this weighty and dreadful threatening, that such vices shut against us the kingdom of God. By appealing to their own knowledge, he intimates that this was no doubtful matter. Some might think it harsh, or inconsistent with the Divine goodness, that all who have incurred the guilt of fornication or covetousness are excluded from the inheritance of the kingdom of heaven. But the answer is easy. Paul does not say that those who have fallen into those sins, and recovered from them, are not pardoned, but pronounces sentence on the sins themselves. After addressing the Corinthians in the same language, he adds:

"And such were some of you; but ye are washed, but ye are sanctified, but ye are justified, in the name of the Lord Jesus, and by the Spirit of our God." (1 Corinthians 6:11.)

When men have repented, and thus give evidence that they are reconciled to God, they are no longer the same persons that they formerly were. But let all fornicators, or unclean or covetous persons, so long as they continue such, be assured that they have no friendship with God, and are deprived of all hope of salvation. It is called the kingdom of Christ and of God, because God hath given it to his Son that we may obtain it through him.

Nor covetous man, who is an idolater. "Covetousness," as he says in another place, "is idolatry," (Colossians 3:5,) — not the idolatry which is so frequently condemned in Scripture, but one of a different description. All covetous men must deny God, and put wealth in his place; such is their blind greediness of wretched gain. But why does Paul attribute to covetousness alone what belongs equally to other carnal passions? In what respect is covetousness better entitled to this disgraceful name than ambition, or than a vain confidence in ourselves? I answer, that this disease is widely spread, and not a few minds have caught the infection. Nay, it is not reckoned a disease, but receives, on the contrary, very general commendation. This accounts for the harshness of Paul's language, which arose from a desire to tear from our hearts the false view.

Verse 6

Let no man deceive you. There have always been ungodly dogs, (156) by whom the threatenings of the prophets were made the subject of merriment and ridicule. We find such characters in our own day. In all ages, indeed, Satan raises up sorcerers of this description, who endeavor by unholy scoffs to escape the Divine judgment, and who actually exercise a kind of fascination over consciences not sufficiently established in the fear of God. "This is a trivial fault. Fornication is viewed by God as a light matter. Under the law of grace God is not so cruel. He has not formed us so as to be our own executioners. The frailty of nature excuses us." These and similar expressions are often used by the scoffers. Paul, on the contrary, exclaims that we must guard against that sophistry by which consciences are ensnared to their ruin.

For because of these things cometh the wrath of God. If we consider the present tense to be here used, agreeably to the Hebrew idiom, for the future, these words are a threatening of the last judgment. But I agree with those who take the word cometh in an indefinite sense, — the word of God usually cometh, — as reminding them of the ordinary judgments of God which were executed before their own eyes. And certainly, if we were not blind and slothful, there are sufficiently numerous examples by which God testifies that he is the just avenger of such crimes, — examples of the pouring out of divine indignation, privately against individuals, and publicly against cities, and kings, and nations.

Upon the children of disobedience, — upon unbelievers or rebels. This expression must not be overlooked. Paul is now addressing believers, and his object is not so much to present alarming views of their own danger, as to rouse them to behold reflected in wicked men, as in mirrors, the dreadful judgments of God. God does not make himself an object of terror to his children, that they may avoid him, but does all that can be done in a fatherly manner, to draw them to himself. They ought to learn this lesson, not to involve themselves in a dangerous fellowship with the ungodly, whose ruin is thus foreseen.

Verse 8

For ye were once darkness. The precepts which immediately follow derive greater weight from the motives with which they are mingled. Having spoken of unbelievers, and warned the Ephesians not to become partakers of their crimes and their

98

destruction, he argues still further, that they ought to differ widely from the life and conduct of those men. At the same time, in order to guard them against ingratitude to God, he refreshes their remembrance of their own past life. "You ought," he says, "to be very different persons from what you formerly were; for out of darkness God hath made you light." Darkness is the name here given to the whole nature of man before regeneration; for, where the brightness of God does not shine, there is nothing but fearful darkness. Light, again, is the name given to those who are enlightened by the Spirit of God; for immediately afterwards in the same sense, he calls them children of light, and draws the inference, that they ought to walk in light, because by the mercy of God they had been rescued from darkness. Observe here, we are said to belight in the Lord, because, while we are out of Christ, all is under the dominion of Satan, whom we know to be the Prince of darkness.

Verse 9

For the fruit of the light. (157) This parenthesis is introduced, to point out the road in which the children of light ought to walk. A complete description is not given, but a few parts of a holy and pious life are introduced by way of example. To give them a general view of duty, their attention is again directed to the will of God. Whoever desires to live in a proper and safe manner, let him resolve to obey God, and to take his will as the rule. To regulate life entirely by his command is, as he says in another Epistle, a reasonable service, (Romans 12:1,) or, as another inspired man expresses it, To obey is better than sacrifice. (1 Samuel 15:22.) I wonder how the word Spirit (πνεύματος) has crept into many Greek manuscripts, as the other reading is more consistent, — the fruit of the light Paul's meaning indeed is not affected; for in either case it will be this, that believers must walk in the light, because they are "children of the light." This is done, when they do not live according to their own will, but devote themselves entirely to obedience to God, — when they undertake nothing but by his command. Besides, such obedience is testified by its fruits, such as goodness, righteousness, and truth.

Verse 11

And have no fellowship. As "the children of light" dwell amidst the darkness, or, in other words, in the midst of "a perverse and crooked generation," (Deuteronomy 32:5,) — there is good reason for warning them to keep themselves apart from wicked actions. It is not enough that we do not, of our own accord, undertake anything wicked. We must beware of joining or assisting those who do wrong. In short, we must abstain from giving any consent, or advice, or approbation, or assistance; for in all these ways we have fellowship. And lest any one should imagine that he has done his duty, merely by not conniving, he adds, but rather reprove them. (158) Such a course is opposed to all dissimulation. Where a manifest offense is committed against God, every man will be eager to vindicate himself from any share in the guilt, but very few will guard against connivance; nearly all will practice some kind of dissimulation. But rather than the truth of God shall not remain unshaken, let a hundred worlds perish.

The word ἐλέγχειν, which is translated reprove, answers to the metaphor of darkness; for it literally signifies to drag forth to the light what was formerly unknown. As ungodly men flatter themselves in their vices, (Psalms 36:2,) and wish their crimes to be concealed, or to be reckoned virtues, Paul enjoins that they shall be reproved. He calls them unfruitful; because they not only do no good, but are absolutely hurtful.

Verse 12

Which are done by them in secret. This shews the advantage of reproving the ungodly. If they do but escape the eyes of men, there is no crime, however shocking to be mentioned, which they will not perpetrate. To use a common proverb, "Night has no shame." What is the reason of this? Sunk in the darkness of ignorance, they neither see their own baseness, nor think that it is seen by God and by angels. But let the torch of God's word be brought forward, and their eyes are opened. Then they begin to blush and be ashamed. By their advices and reproofs the saints enlighten blind unbelievers, and drag forth from their concealment to the light of day those who were sunk in ignorance.

When unbelievers keep the doors of their houses shut, and withdraw from the view of men, it is a shame even to speak of the baseness and wickedness with which they rush into all manner of licentiousness. Would they thus lay aside all shame, and give loose reins to their passions, if darkness did not give them courage, — if they did not entertain the hope that what is hidden will pass unpunished? But do you, by reproving them, bring forward the light, that they may be ashamed of their own baseness. Such shame, arising from an acknowledgment of baseness, is the first step to repentance.

"If there come in one that believeth not, or one unlearned, he is convinced of all, he is judged of all; and thus are the secrets of his heart made manifest; and so, falling down on his face, he worships God" (1 Corinthians 14:24.)

It may be thought that the word is used here in an unusual acceptation. Erasmus, by substituting another word forreprove, has destroyed the whole meaning; for Paul's object is to shew that it will not be without advantage if the works of unbelievers are reproved.

Verse 13

But when all things are reproved. As the participle, (φανερούμενον,) which is translated,that which doth make manifest, is in the middle voice, it admits either of a passive or active signification. It may be either rendered, that which is made manifest, or that which doth make manifest. If the passive signification, which is followed by the ancient translator, be preferred, the word light will denote, as formerly, that which gives light, and the meaning will be, that evil works, which had been concealed, will stand out to public view, when they have been made manifest by the word of God: If the participle be taken actively, there will still be two ways of expounding it: 1. Whatever manifests is light; 2. That which manifests anything or all things, is light; taking the singular as put for the plural number. There is no difficulty, as Erasmus dreaded, about the article; for the apostles are not in the habit of adhering very strictly to rule about placing every article, and even among elegant writers this mode of using it would be allowable. The context appears to me to shew clearly that this is Paul's meaning. He had exhorted them to reprove the evil works of unbelievers, and thus to drag them out of darkness; and he now adds, that what he enjoins upon them is the proper business of light — to make manifest It is Light, he says, which makes all things manifest; and hence it followed that they were unworthy of the name, if they did not bring to light what was involved in darkness.

Verse 14

Wherefore he saith. Interpreters are at great pains to discover the passage of Scripture which Paul appears to quote, and which is nowhere to be found. I shall state my opinion. He first exhibits Christ as speaking by his ministers; for this is the ordinary message which is every day delivered by preachers of the gospel. What other object do they propose than to raise the dead to life?

"The hour is coming, and now is, when the dead shall hear the voice of the Son of God, and they that hear shall live"
(John 5:25.)

Let us now attend to the context. "Unbelievers," Paul had said, "must be reproved, that, being brought forth to the light, they may begin to acknowledge their wickedness." He therefore represents Christ as uttering a voice which is constantly heard in the preaching of the gospel,

Arise, thou that sleepest. The allusion, I have no doubt, is to the prophecies which relate to Christ's kingdom; such as that of Isaiah,

"Arise, shine; for thy light is come, and the glory of Jehovah
is risen upon thee" (Isaiah 60:1.)

Let us therefore endeavor, as far as lies in our power, to rouse the sleeping and dead, that we may bring them to the light of Christ.

And Christ shall give thee light. This does not mean that, when we have risen from death to life, his light begins to shine upon us, as if our performances came before his grace. All that is intended is to show that, when Christ enlightens us, we rise from death to life, — and thus to confirm the former statement, that unbelievers must be recovered from their blindness, in order to be saved. Instead of ἐπιφαύσει, he shall give light, some copies read ἐφάψεται, he shall touch; but this reading is an evident blunder, and may be dismissed without any argument. (159)

Verse 15

See then. If believers must not neglect to drive away the darkness of others by their own brightness, how much less ought they to be blind as to their own conduct in life? What darkness shall conceal those on whom Christ, the Sun of righteousness, has arisen? Placed, as it were, in a crowded theater, they ought to live under the eye of God and of angels. Let them stand in awe of these witnesses, though they may be concealed from the view of all mortals. Dismissing the metaphor of darkness and light, he enjoins them to regulate their life circumspectly as wise men, (160) who have been educated by the Lord in the school of true wisdom. Our understanding must shew itself by taking God for our guide and instructor, to teach us his own will.

Verse 16

Redeeming the time. By a consideration of the time he enforces his exhortation. The days are evil. Everything around us tends to corrupt and mislead; so that it is difficult for godly persons, who walk among so many thorns, to escape unhurt. Such corruption having infected the age, the devil appears to have obtained tyrannical sway; so that time cannot be dedicated to God without being in some way redeemed. And what shall be the price of its redemption? To withdraw from the endless variety of allurements which would easily lead us astray; to rid ourselves from the cares and pleasures of the world; and, in a word, to abandon every hinderance. Let us be eager to recover it in every possible way, and let the numerous offenses and arduous toil, which many are in the habit of alleging as an apology for indolence, serve rather to awaken our vigilance.

Verse 17

Wherefore be ye not unwise. He whose

"delight is in the law of the Lord, and who meditates in it day and night," (Psalms 1:2,)

will triumph over every obstacle which Satan can oppose to his progress. Whence comes it that some wander, others fall, others strike against a rock, others go away, — but because we allow ourselves to be gradually blinded by Satan, and lose sight of the will of God, which we ought constantly to remember? And observe, that Paul defines wisdom to be, understanding what the will of the Lord is

"How shall a young man," says David, "direct his way? By attending to thy word, O Lord." (Psalms 119:9.)

He speaks of youths, but it is the same wisdom which belongs to old men.

Verse 18

And be not drunk with wine. When he enjoins them not to be drunk, he forbids excessive and immoderate drinking of every description. "Be not intemperate in drinking."

In which (161) is lasciviousness. The Greek word ἀσωτία, which is translated "lasciviousness," points out the evils which arise from drunkenness. I understand by it all that is implied in a wanton and dissolute life; for to translate it luxury, would quite enfeeble the sense. The meaning therefore is, that drunkards throw off quickly every restraint of modesty or shame; that where wine reigns, profligacy naturally follows; and consequently, that all who have any regard to moderation or decency ought to avoid and abhor drunkenness.

The children of this world are accustomed to indulge in deep drinking as an excitement to mirth. Such carnal excitement is contrasted with that holy joy of which the Spirit of God is the Author, and which produces entirely opposite effects. To what does drunkenness lead? To unbounded licentiousness, — to unbridled, indecent merriment. And to what does spiritual joy lead, when it is most strongly excited? (162)

Verse 19

To psalms, and hymns, and spiritual songs. These are truly pleasant and delightful fruits. The Spirit means "joy in the Holy Ghost," (Romans 14:17;) and the exhortation, be ye filled, (ver. 18,) alludes to deep drinking, with which it is indirectly contrasted. Speaking to themselves, is speaking among themselves. Nor does he enjoin them to sing inwardly or alone; for he immediately adds, singing in your hearts; as if he had said, "Let your praises be not merely on the tongue, as hypocrites do, but from the heart." What may be the exact difference between psalms and hymns, or between hymns and songs, it is not easy to determine, though a few remarks on this subject shall be offered on a future occasion. (163) The appellation spiritual, given to these songs, is strikingly appropriate; for the songs most frequently used are almost always on trifling subjects, and very far from being chaste.

Verse 20

Giving thanks always. He means that this is a pleasure which ought never to lose its relish; that this is an exercise of which we ought never to weary. Innumerable benefits which we receive from God yield fresh cause of joy and thanksgiving. At the same time, he reminds believers that it will argue ungodly and disgraceful sloth, if they shall not always give thanks, — if their whole life shall not be spent in the study and exercise of praising God.

Verse 21

Submit yourselves. God has bound us so strongly to each other, that no man ought to endeavor to avoid subjection; and where love reigns, mutual services will be rendered. I do not except even kings and governors, whose very authority is held for the service of the community. It is highly proper that all should be exhorted to be subject to each other in their turn.

But as nothing is more irksome to the mind of man than this mutual subjection, he directs us to the fear of Christ, who alone can subdue our fierceness, that we may not refuse the yoke, and can humble our pride, that we may not be ashamed of serving our neighbors. It does not much affect the sense, whether we interpret the fear of Christ, passively, thus, — let us submit to our neighbors, because we fear Christ; or actively, — let us submit to them, because the minds of all godly persons ought to be influenced by such fear under the reign of Christ. Some Greek manuscripts read, "the fear of God. " The change may have been introduced by some person, who thought that the other phrase, the fear of Christ, though by far the most appropriate, sounded a little harsh. (164)

Verse 22

Wives, submit yourselves. He comes now to the various conditions of life; for, besides the universal bond of subjection, some are more closely bound to each other, according to their respective callings. The community at large is divided, as it were, into so many yokes, out of which arises mutual obligation. There is, first, the yoke of marriage between husband and wife; — secondly, the yoke which binds parents and children; — and, thirdly, the yoke which connects masters and servants. By this arrangement there are six different classes, for each of whom Paul lays down peculiar duties. He begins with wives, whom he enjoins to be subject to their husbands, in the same manner as to Christ, — as to the Lord. Not that the authority is equal, but wives cannot obey Christ without yielding obedience to their husbands.

Verse 23

For the husband is the head of the wife. This is the reason assigned why wives should be obedient. Christ has appointed the same relation to exist between a husband and a wife, as between himself and his church. This comparison ought to produce a stronger impression on their minds, than the mere declaration that such is the appointment of God. Two things are here stated. God has given to the husband authority over the wife; and a resemblance of this authority is found in Christ, who is the head of the church, as the husband is of the wife.

And he is the savior of the body. The pronoun HE (αὐτός) is supposed by some to refer to Christ; and, by others, to the husband. It applies more naturally, in my opinion, to Christ, but still with a view to the present subject. In this point, as well as in others, the resemblance ought to hold. As Christ rules over his church for her salvation, so nothing yields more advantage or comfort to the wife than to be subject to her husband. To refuse that subjection, by means of which they might be saved, is to choose destruction.

Verse 24

But, as the church is subject to Christ. The particle but, may lead some to believe that the words, he is the savior of the body, are intended to anticipate an objection. Christ has, no doubt, this peculiar claim, that he is the Savior of the Church: nevertheless, let wives know, that their husbands, though they cannot produce equal claims, have authority over them, after the example of Christ. I prefer the former interpretation; for the argument derived from the word but, (ἀλλά,) does not appear to me to have much weight.

Verse 25

Husbands, love your wives. From husbands, on the other hand, the apostle requires that they cherish toward their wives no ordinary love; for to them, also, he holds out the example of Christ, — even as Christ also loved the church. If they are honored to bear his image, and to be, in some measure, his representatives, they ought to resemble him also in the discharge of duty.

And gave himself for it. This is intended to express the strong affection which husbands ought to have for their wives, though he takes occasion, immediately afterwards, to commend the grace of Christ. Let husbands imitate Christ in this respect, that he scrupled not to die for his church. One peculiar consequence, indeed, which resulted from his death, — that by it he redeemed his church, — is altogether beyond the power of men to imitate.

Verse 26

That he might sanctify, — or, that he might separate it to himself; for such I consider to be the meaning of the word sanctify This is accomplished by the forgiveness of sins, and the regeneration of the Spirit.

Washing it with the washing of water. Having mentioned the inward and hidden sanctification, he now adds the outward symbol, by which it is visibly confirmed; as if he had said, that a pledge of that sanctification is held out to us by baptism. Here it is necessary to guard against unsound interpretation, lest the wicked superstition of men, as has frequently happened, change a sacrament into an idol. When Paul says that we are washed by baptism, his meaning is, that God employs it for declaring to us that we are washed, and at the same time performs what it represents. If the truth — or, which is the same thing, the exhibition of the truth — were not connected with baptism, it would be improper to say that baptism is the washing of the soul. At the same time, we must beware of ascribing to the sign, or to the minister, what belongs to God alone. We must not imagine that washing is performed by the minister, or that water cleanses the pollutions of the soul, which nothing but the blood of Christ can accomplish. In short, we must beware of giving any portion of our confidence to the element or to man; for the true and proper use of the sacrament is to lead us directly to Christ, and to place all our dependence upon him.

Others again suppose that too much importance is given to the sign, by saying that baptism is the washing of the soul. Under the influence of this fear, they labor exceedingly to lessen the force of the eulogium which is here pronounced on baptism. But they are manifestly wrong; for, in the first place, the apostle does not say that it is the sign which washes, but declares it to be exclusively the work of God. It is God who washes, and the honor of performing it cannot lawfully be taken from its Author and given to the sign. But there is no absurdity in saying that God employs a sign as the outward means. Not that the power of God is limited by the sign, but this assistance is accommodated to the weakness of our capacity. Some are offended at this view, imagining that it takes from the Holy Spirit a work which is peculiarly his own, and which is everywhere ascribed to him in Scripture. But they are mistaken; for God acts by the sign in such a manner, that its whole efficacy depends upon his Spirit. Nothing more is attributed to the sign than to be an inferior organ, utterly useless in itself, except so far as it derives its power from another source.

Equally groundless is their fear, that by this interpretation the freedom of God will be restrained. The grace of God is not confined to the sign; so that God may not, if he pleases, bestow it without the aid of the sign. Besides, many receive the sign who are not made partakers of grace; for the sign is common to all, to the good and to the bad alike; but the Spirit is bestowed on none but the elect, and the sign, as we have said, has no efficacy without the Spirit. The Greek participle καθαρίσας, is in the past tense, as if he had said, "After having washed." But, as the Latin language has no active participle in the past tense, I chose rather to disregard this, and to translate it (mundans) washing, instead of (mundatam) having been washed; which would have kept out of view a matter of far greater importance, namely, that to God alone belongs the work of cleansing.

In the word. (165) This is very far from being a superfluous addition; for, if the word is taken away, the whole power of the sacraments is gone. What else are the sacraments but seals of the word? This single consideration will drive away superstition. How comes it that superstitious men are confounded by signs, but because their minds are not directed to the Word, which would lead them to God? Certainly, when we look to anything else than to the word, there is nothing sound, nothing pure; but one absurdity springs out of another, till at length the signs, which were appointed by God for the salvation of men, become profane, and degenerate into gross idolatry. The only difference, therefore, between the sacraments of the godly and the contrivances of unbelievers, is found in the Word.

By the Word is here meant the promise, which explains the value and use of the signs. Hence it appears, that the Papists do not at all observe the signs in a proper manner. They boast indeed, of having "the Word," but appear to regard it as a sort of enchantment; for they mutter it in an unknown tongue; as if it were addressed to dead matter, and not to men. No explanation of the mystery is made to the people; and in this respect, were there no other, the sacrament begins to be nothing more than the dead element of water.In the word is equivalent to "By the word."

Verse 27

That he might present it to himself. He declares what is the design of baptism and of our being washed. It is, that we may live in a holy and unblamable manner before God. We are washed by Christ, not that we may return to our pollution, but that we may retain through our life the purity which we have once received. This is described in metaphorical language appropriate to his argument.

Not having spot or wrinkle. As the beauty of the wife produces love in the husband, so Christ adorns the Church his bride with holiness as a proof of his regard. This metaphor contains an allusion to marriage; but he afterwards lays aside the figure, and says plainly, that Christ has reconciled the church, that it might be holy and without blemish. The true beauty of the church consists in this conjugal chastity, that is, in holiness and purity.

The word present (παραστήσ°Y) implies that the church ought to be holy, not only in the view of men, but in the eyes of the Lord; for Paul says, that he might present it to himself, not that he might shew it to others, though the fruits of that hidden purity become afterwards evident in outward works. Pelagians were wont to quote this passage in order to prove the perfection of righteousness in this life, but have been successfully answered by Augustine. Paul does not state what has been done, but for what purpose Christ has cleansed his church. Now, when a thing is said to be done that another may afterwards follow, it is idle to conclude that this latter thing, which ought to follow, has been already done. We do not deny that the holiness of the church is already begun; but, so long as there is daily progress, there cannot be perfection.

Verse 28

He that loveth his wife. An argument is now drawn from nature itself, to prove that men ought to love their wives. Every man, by his very nature, loves himself. But no man can love himself without loving his wife. Therefore, the man who does not love his wife is a monster. The minor proposition is proved in this manner. Marriage was appointed by God on the condition that the two should be one flesh; and that this unity may be the more sacred, he again recommends it to our notice by the consideration of Christ and his church. Such is the amount of his argument, which to a certain extent applies universally to human society. To shew what man owes to man, Isaiah says, "hide not thyself from thine own flesh." (Isaiah 58:7.) But this refers to our common nature. Between a man and his wife there is a far closer relation; for they not only are united by a resemblance of nature, but by the bond of marriage have become one man. Whoever considers seriously the design of marriage cannot but love his wife.

Verse 29

Even as Christ the church. He proceeds to enforce the obligations of marriage by representing to us Christ and his Church; for a more powerful example could not have been adduced. The strong affection which a husband ought to cherish towards his wife is exemplified by Christ, and an instance of that unity which belongs to marriage is declared to exist between himself and the Church. This is a remarkable passage on the mysterious intercourse which we have with Christ.

Verse 30

For we are members of his body, of his flesh, and of his bones. First, this is no exaggeration, but the simple truth. Secondly, he does not simply mean that Christ is a partaker of our nature, but expresses something higher (καὶ ἐμφατικώτερον) and more emphatic.

Verse 31

For this cause. This is an exact quotation from the writings of Moses. (Genesis 2:24.) And what does it mean? As Eve was formed out of the substance of her husband, and thus was a part of himself; so, if we are the true members of Christ, we share his substance, and by this intercourse unite into one body. In short, Paul describes our union to Christ, a symbol and pledge of which is given to us in the ordinance of the supper. Those who talk about the torture exercised on this passage to make it refer to the Lord's supper, while no mention is made of the supper, but of marriage, are egregiously mistaken. When they admit that the death of Christ is commemorated in the supper, but not that such intercourse exists as we assert from the words of Christ, we quote this passage against them. Paul says that we are members of his flesh and of his bones. Do we wonder then, that in the Lord's supper he holds out his body to be enjoyed by us, and to nourish us unto eternal life? Thus we prove that the only union which we maintain to be represented by the Lord's supper is here declared in its truth and consequences by the apostle.

Two subjects are exhibited together; for the spiritual union between Christ and his church is so treated as to illustrate the common law of marriage, to which the quotation from Moses relates. He immediately adds, that the saying is fulfilled in Christ and the church. Every opportunity which presents itself for proclaiming our obligations to Christ is readily embraced, but he adapts his illustration of them to the present subject. It is uncertain whether Moses introduces Adam as using these words, or gives them as an inference drawn by himself from the creation of man. Nor is it of much consequence which of these views be taken; for, in either case, we must hold it to be an announcement of the will of God, enjoining the duties which men owe to their wives.

He shall leave his father and mother. As if he had said, "Let him rather leave his father and mother than not cleave to his wife." The marriage bond does not set aside the other duties of mankind, nor are the commandments of God so inconsistent with each other, that a man cannot be a good and faithful husband without ceasing to be a dutiful son. It is altogether a question of degree. Moses draws the comparison, in order to express more strongly the close and sacred union which subsists between husband and wife. A son is bound by an inviolable law of nature to perform his duties towards his father; and when the obligations of a husband towards his wife are declared to be stronger, their force is the better understood. He who resolves to be a good husband will not fail to perform his filial duties, but will regard marriage as more sacred than all other ties.

And they two shall be one flesh. They shall be one man, or, to use a common phrase, they shall constitute one person; which certainly would not hold true with regard to any other kind of relationship. All depends on this, that the wife was formed

110

of the flesh and bones of her husband. Such is the union between us and Christ, who in some sort makes us partakers of his substance. "We are bone of his bone, and flesh of his flesh," (Genesis 2:23;) not because, like ourselves, he has a human nature, but because, by the power of his Spirit, he makes us a part of his body, so that from him we derive our life.

Verse 32

This is a great mystery. He concludes by expressing his astonishment at the spiritual union between Christ and the church. This is a great mystery; by which he means, that no language can explain fully what it implies. It is to no purpose that men fret themselves to comprehend, by the judgment of the flesh, the manner and character of this union; for here the infinite power of the Divine Spirit is exerted. Those who refuse to admit anything on this subject beyond what their own capacity can reach, act an exceedingly foolish part. We tell them that the flesh and blood of Christ are exhibited to us in the Lord's supper. "Explain to us the manner," they reply, "or you will not convince us." For my own part, I am overwhelmed by the depth of this mystery, and am not ashamed to join Paul in acknowledging at once my ignorance and my admiration. How much more satisfactory would this be than to follow my carnal judgment, in undervaluing what Paul declares to be a deep mystery! Reason itself teaches how we ought to act in such matters; for whatever is supernatural is clearly beyond our own comprehension. Let us therefore labor more to feel Christ living in us, than to discover the nature of that intercourse.

We cannot avoid admiring the acuteness of the Papists, who conclude from the word mystery (μυστήριον) that marriage is one of seven sacraments, as if they had the power of changing water into wine. They enumerate seven sacraments, while Christ has instituted no more than two; and, to prove that matrimony is one of the seven, they produce this passage. On what ground? Because the Vulgate has adopted the word Sacrament (sacramentum) as a translation of the word Mystery, which the apostle uses. As if Sacrament (sacramentum) did not frequently, among Latin writers, denote Mystery, or as if Mystery had not been the word employed by Paul in the same Epistle, when speaking of the calling of the Gentiles. But the present question is, Has marriage been appointed as a sacred symbol of the grace of God, to declare and represent to us something spiritual, such as Baptism or the Lord's Supper? They have no ground for such an assertion, unless it be that they have been deceived by the doubtful signification of a Latin word, or rather by their ignorance of the Greek language. If the simple fact had been observed, that the word used by Paul is Mystery, no mistake would ever have occurred.

We see then the hammer and anvil with which they fabricated this sacrament. But they have given another proof of their indolence in not attending to the correction which is immediately added,

But I speak concerning Christ and the church. He intended to give express warning that no man should understand him as speaking of marriage; so that his meaning is more fully expressed than if he had uttered the former sentiment without any exception. The great mystery is, that Christ breathes into the church his own life and power. But who would discover here anything like a sacrament? This blunder arose from the grossest ignorance.

Verse 33

Nevertheless, let every one. Having digressed a little from this subject, though the very digression aided his design, he adopts the method usually followed in short precepts, by giving a brief summary of duties. Husbands are required to love their wives, and wives to fear (φοβῶται) their husbands, understanding by fear that reverence which will lead them to be submissive. Where reverence does not exist, there will be no willing subjection. (166)

CALVIN EPHESIANS 6

Verse 1

Children, obey. Why does the apostle use the word obey instead of honor, (167) which has a greater extent of meaning? It is because Obedience is the evidence of that honor which children owe to their parents, and is therefore more earnestly enforced. It is likewise more difficult; for the human mind recoils from the idea of subjection, and with difficulty allows itself to be placed under the control of another. Experience shews how rare this virtue is; for do we find one among a thousand that is obedient to his parents? By a figure of speech, a part is here put for the whole, but it is the most important part, and is necessarily accompanied by all the others.

In the Lord. Besides the law of nature, which is acknowledged by all nations, the obedience of children is enforced by the authority of God. Hence it follows, that parents are to be obeyed, so far only as is consistent with piety to God, which comes first in order. If the command of God is the rule by which the submission of children is to be regulated, it would be foolish to suppose that the performance of this duty could lead away from God himself.

For this is right. This is added in order to restrain the fierceness which, we have already said, appears to be natural to almost all men. He proves it to be right, because God has commanded it; for we are not at liberty to dispute, or call in question, the appointment of him whose will is the unerring rule of goodness and righteousness. That honor should be represented as including obedience is not surprising; for mere ceremony is of no value in the sight of God. The precept, honor thy father and mother, comprehends all the duties by which the sincere affection and respect of children to their parents can be expressed.

Verse 2

Which is the first commandment with promise. The promises annexed to the commandments are intended to excite our hopes, and to impart a greater cheerfulness to our obedience; and therefore Paul uses this as a kind of seasoning to render the submission, which he enjoins on children, more pleasant and agreeable. He does not merely say, that God has offered a reward to him who obeys his father and mother, but that such an offer is peculiar to this commandment. If each of the commandments had its own promises, there would have been no ground for the commendation bestowed in the present instance. But this is the first commandment, Paul tells us, which God has been pleased, as it were, to seal by a remarkable promise. There is some difficulty here; for the second commandment likewise contains a promise,

"I am the Lord thy God, who shew mercy unto thousands of them that love me, and keep my commandments."
(Exodus 20:5.)

But this is universal, applying indiscriminately to the whole law, and cannot be said to be annexed to that commandment. Paul's assertion still holds true, that no other commandment but that which enjoins the obedience due by children to their parents is distinguished by a promise.

Verse 3

That it may be well with thee. The promise is — a long life; from which we are led to understand that the present life is not to be overlooked among the gifts of God. On this and other kindred subjects I must refer my reader to the Institutes of the Christian Religion; (168) satisfying myself at present with saying, in a few words, that the reward promised to the obedience of children is highly appropriate. Those who shew kindness to their parents from whom they derived life, are assured by God, that in this life it will be well with them.

And that thou mayest live long on the earth. Moses expressly mentions the land of Canaan,

"that thy days may be long upon the land which
the Lord thy God giveth thee." (Exodus 20:12.)

Beyond this the Jews could not conceive of any life more happy or desirable. But as the same divine blessing is extended to the whole world, Paul has properly left out the mention of a place, the peculiar distinction of which lasted only till the coming of Christ.

Verse 4

And, ye fathers. Parents, on the other hand, are exhorted not to irritate their children by unreasonable severity. This would excite hatred, and would lead them to throw off the yoke altogether. Accordingly, in writing to the Colossians, he adds, "lest they be discouraged." (Colossians 3:21.) Kind and liberal treatment has rather a tendency to cherish reverence for their parents, and to increase the cheerfulness and activity of their obedience, while a harsh and unkind manner rouses them to obstinacy, and destroys the natural affections. But Paul goes on to say, "let them be fondly

115

cherished;" for the Greek word, (ἐκτρέφετε,) which is translated bring up,

unquestionably conveys the idea of gentleness and forbearance. To guard them, however, against the opposite and frequent evil of excessive indulgence, he again draws the rein which he had slackened, and adds, in the instruction and reproof of the Lord. It is not the will of God that parents, in the exercise of kindness, shall spare and corrupt their children. Let their conduct towards their children be at once mild and considerate, so as to guide them in the fear of the Lord, and correct them also when they go astray. That age is so apt to become wanton, that it requires frequent admonition and restraint.

Verse 5

Servants, be obedient. His exhortation to servants is so much the more earnest, on account of the hardship and bitterness of their condition, which renders it more difficult to be endured. And he does not speak merely of outward obedience, but says more about fear willingly rendered; for it is a very rare occurrence to find one who willingly yields himself to the control of another. The servants (δοῦλοι) whom he immediately addresses were not hired servants, like those of the present day, but slaves, such as were in ancient times, whose slavery was perpetual, unless, through the favor of their masters, they obtained freedom, — whom their masters bought with money, that they might impose upon them the most degrading employments, and might, with the full protection of the law, exercise over them the power of life and death. To such he says, obey your masters, lest they should vainly imagine that carnal freedom had been procured for them by the gospel.

But as some of the worst men were compelled by the dread of punishment, he distinguishes between Christian and ungodly servants, by the feelings which they cherished.With fear and trembling; that is, with the careful respect which springs from an honest purpose. It can hardly be expected, however, that so much deference will be paid to a mere man, unless a higher authority shall enforce the obligation; and therefore he adds,as doing the will of God. (Ver. 6.) Hence it follows, that it is not enough if their obedience satisfy the eyes of men; for God requires truth and sincerity of heart. When they serve their masters faithfully, they obey God. As if he had said, "Do not suppose that by the judgment of men you were thrown into slavery. It is God who has laid upon you this burden, who has placed you in the power of your masters. He who conscientiously endeavors to render what he owes to his master, performs his duty not to man only, but to God."

Verse 7

With good will doing service. (Ver. 7.) This is contrasted with the suppressed indignation which swells the bosom of slaves. Though they dare not openly break out or give signs of obstinacy, their dislike of the authority exercised over them is so strong, that it is with the greatest unwillingness and reluctance that they obey their masters.

Whoever reads the accounts of the dispositions and conduct of slaves, which are scattered through the writings of the ancients, will be at no loss to perceive that the number of injunctions here given does not exceed that of the diseases which prevailed among this class, and which it was of importance to cure. But the same instruction applies to male and female servants of our own times. It is God who appoints and regulates all the arrangements of society. As the condition of servants is much more agreeable than that of slaves in ancient times, they ought to consider themselves far less excusable, if they do not endeavor, in every way, to comply with Paul's injunctions.

Masters according to the flesh. (Ver. 5.) This expression is used to soften the harsh aspect of slavery. He reminds them that their spiritual freedom, which was by far the most desirable, remained untouched.

Eye-service (ὀφθαλμοδουλεία) is mentioned; because almost all servants are addicted to flattery, but, as soon as their master's back is turned, indulge freely in contempt, or perhaps in ridicule. Paul therefore enjoins godly persons to keep at the greatest distance from such deceitful pretences.

Verse 8

Knowing that whatsoever good thing any man doeth. What a powerful consolation! However unworthy, however ungrateful or cruel, their masters may be, God will accept their services as rendered to himself. When servants take into account the pride and arrogance of their masters, they often become more indolent from the thought that their labor is thrown away. But Paul informs them that their reward is laid up with God for services which appear to be ill bestowed on unfeeling men; and that there is no reason, therefore, why they should be led aside from the path of duty. He adds, whether bond or free No distinction is made between a slave and a free man. The world is wont to set little value on the labors of slaves; but God esteems them as highly as the duties of kings. In his estimate, the outward station is thrown aside, and each is judged according to the uprightness of his heart.

Verse 9

And ye masters. In the treatment of their slaves, the laws granted to masters a vast amount of power. Whatever had thus been sanctioned by the civil code was regarded by many as in itself lawful. To such an extent did their cruelty in some instances proceed, that the Roman emperors were forced to restrain their tyranny. But though no royal edicts had ever been issued for the protection of slaves, God allows to masters no power over them beyond what is consistent with the law of love. When philosophers attempt to give to the principles of equity their full effect in restraining the excess of severity to slaves, they inculcate that masters ought to treat them in the same manner as hired servants. But they never look beyond utility; and, in judging even of that, they inquire only what is advantageous to the head of the family, or conducive to good order. The Apostle proceeds on a very different principle. He lays down what is lawful according to the Divine appointment, and how far they, too, are debtors to their servants.

Do the same things to them. "Perform the duty which on your part you owe to them." What he calls in another Epistle, (τὸ δίκαιον καὶ τὴν ἰσότητα) that which is just and equal, (169) is precisely what, in this passage, he calls the same things, (τὰ αὐτὰ.) And what is this but the law of analogy? Masters and servants are not indeed on the same level; but there is a mutual law which binds them. By this law, servants are placed under the authority of their masters; and, by the same law, due regard being had to the difference of their station, masters lie under certain obligations to their servants. This analogy is greatly misunderstood; because men do not try it by the law of love, which is the only true standard. Such is the import of Paul's phrase, the same things; for we are all ready enough to demand what is due to ourselves; but, when our own duty comes to be performed, every one attempts to plead exemption. It is chiefly, however, among persons of authority and rank that injustice of this sort prevails.

Forbearing threatenings. Every expression of disdain, arising from the pride of masters, is included in the single word, threatenings. They are charged not to assume a lordly air or a terrific attitude, as if they were constantly threatening some evil against their servants, when they have occasion to address them. Threatenings, and every kind of barbarity, originate in this, that masters look upon their servants as if they had been born for their sake alone, and treat them as if they were of no more value than cattle. Under this one description, Paul forbids every kind of disdainful and barbarous treatment.

Their Master and yours. A very necessary warning. What is there which we will not dare to attempt against our inferiors, if they have no ability to resist, and no means of obtaining redress, — if no avenger, no protector appears, none who will be moved by compassion to listen to their complaints? It happens here, in short, according to the common proverb, that Impunity is the mother of Licentiousness. But Paul here reminds them, that, while masters possess authority over their servants, they have themselves the same Master in heaven, to whom they must render an account.

And there is no respect of persons with him. A regard to persons blinds our eyes, so as to leave no room for law or justice; but Paul affirms that it is of no value in the sight of God. By person is meant anything about a man which does not belong to the real question, and which we take into account in forming a judgment. Relationship, beauty, rank, wealth, friendship, and everything of this sort, gain our favor; while the opposite qualities produce contempt and sometimes hatred. As those absurd feelings arising from the sight of a person have the greatest possible influence on human judgments, those who are invested with power are apt to flatter themselves, as if God would countenance such corruptions. "Who is he that God should regard him, or defend his interest against mine?" Paul, on the contrary, informs masters that they are mistaken if they suppose that their servants will be of little or no account before God, because they are so before men. "God is no respecter of persons," (Acts 10:34,) and the cause of the meanest man will not be a whit less regarded by him than that of the loftiest monarch.

Verse 10

Finally. Resuming his general exhortations, he again enjoins them to be strong, — to summon up courage and vigor; for there is always much to enfeeble us, and we are ill fitted to resist. But when our weakness is considered, an exhortation like this would have no effect, unless the Lord were present, and stretched out his hand to render assistance, or rather, unless he supplied us with all the power. Paul therefore adds, in the Lord. As if he had said, "'You have no right to reply, that you have not the ability; for all that I require of you is, be strong in the Lord. " To explain his meaning more fully, he adds, in the power of his might, which tends greatly to increase our confidence, particularly as it shews the remarkable assistance which God usually bestows upon believers. If the Lord aids us by his mighty power, we have no reason to shrink from the combat. But it will be asked, What purpose did it serve to enjoin the Ephesians to be strong in the Lord's mighty power, which they could not of themselves accomplish? I answer, there are two clauses here which must be considered. He exhorts them to be courageous, but at the same time reminds them to ask from God a supply of their own deficiencies, and promises that, in answer to their prayers, the power of God will be displayed.

Verse 11

Put on the whole armor. God has furnished us with various defensive weapons, provided we do not indolently refuse what is offered. But we are almost all chargeable with carelessness and hesitation in using the offered grace; just as if a soldier, about to meet the enemy, should take his helmet, and neglect his shield. To correct this security, or, we should rather say, this indolence, Paul borrows a comparison from the military art, and bids us put on the whole armor of God. We ought to be prepared on all sides, so as to want nothing. The Lord offers to us arms for repelling every kind of attack. It remains for us to apply them to use, and not leave them hanging on the wall. To quicken our vigilance, he reminds us that we must not only engage in open warfare, but that we have a crafty and insidious foe to encounter, who frequently lies in ambush; for such is the import of the apostle's phrase, THE WILES (170) (τὰς μεθοδείας) of the devil

Verse 12

For we wrestle (171) not. To impress them still more deeply with their danger, he points out the nature of the enemy, which he illustrates by a comparative statement, Not against flesh and blood. The meaning is, that our difficulties are far greater than if we had to fight with men. There we resist human strength, sword is opposed to sword, man contends with man, force is met by force, and skill by skill; but here the case is widely different. All amounts to this, that our enemies are such as no human power can withstand. By flesh and blood the apostle denotes men, who are so denominated in order to contrast them with spiritual assailants. This is no bodily struggle.

Let us remember this when the injurious treatment of others provokes us to revenge. Our natural disposition would lead us to direct all our exertions against the men themselves; but this foolish desire will be restrained by the consideration that the men who annoy us are nothing more than darts thrown by the hand of Satan. While we are employed in destroying those darts, we lay ourselves open to be wounded on all sides. To wrestle with flesh and blood will not only be useless, but highly pernicious. We must go straight to the enemy, who attacks and wounds us from his concealment, — who slays before he appears.

But to return to Paul. He describes our enemy as formidable, not to overwhelm us with fear, but to quicken our diligence and earnestness; for there is a middle course to be observed. When the enemy is neglected, he does his utmost to oppress us with sloth, and afterwards disarms us by terror; so that, ere the engagement has commenced, we are vanquished. By speaking of the power of the enemy, Paul labors to keep us more on the alert. He had already called him the devil, but now employs a variety of epithets, to make the reader understand that this is not an enemy who may be safely despised.

Against principalities, against powers. Still, his object in producing alarm is not to fill us with dismay, but to excite us to caution. He calls them κοσμοκράτορας, that is, princes of the world; but he explains himself more fully by adding — of the darkness of the world. The devil reigns in the world, because the world is nothing else than darkness. Hence it follows, that the corruption of the world gives way to the kingdom of the devil; for he could not reside in a pure and upright creature of God, but all arises from the sinfulness of men. By darkness, it is almost unnecessary to say, are meant unbelief and ignorance of God, with the consequences to which they lead. As the whole world is covered with darkness, the devil is called "the prince of this world." (John 14:30.)

By calling it wickedness, he denotes the malignity and cruelty of the devil, and, at the same time, reminds us that the utmost caution is necessary to prevent him from gaining an advantage. For the same reason, the epithet spiritual is applied; for, when the enemy is invisible, our danger is greater. There is emphasis, too, in the phrase, in heavenly places; for the elevated station from which the attack is made gives us greater trouble and difficulty.

An argument drawn from this passage by the Manicheans, to support their wild notion of two principles, is easily refuted. They supposed the devil to be (ἀντίθεον) an antagonist deity, whom the righteous God would not subdue without great exertion. For Paul does not ascribe to devils a principality, which they seize without the consent, and maintain in spite of the opposition, of the Divine Being, — but a principality which, as Scripture everywhere asserts, God, in righteous judgment, yields to them over the wicked. The inquiry is, not what power they have in opposition to God, but how far they ought to excite our alarm, and keep us on our guard. Nor is any countenance here given to the belief, that the devil has formed, and keeps for himself, the middle region of the air. Paul does not assign to them a fixed territory, which they can call their own, but merely intimates that they are engaged in hostility, and occupy an elevated station.

Verse 13

Wherefore take unto you. Though our enemy is so powerful, Paul does not infer that we must throw away our spears, but that we must prepare our minds for the battle. A promise of victory is, indeed, involved in the exhortation, that ye may be able. If we only put on the whole armor of God, and fight valiantly to the end, we shall certainly stand. On any other supposition, we would be discouraged by the number and variety of the contests; and therefore he adds, in the evil day. By this expression he rouses them from security, bids them prepare themselves for hard, painful, and dangerous conflicts, and, at the same time, animates them with the hope of victory; for amidst the greatest dangers they will be safe. And having done all. They are thus directed to cherish confidence through the whole course of life. There will be no danger which may not be successfully met by the power of God; nor will any who, with this assistance, fight against Satan, fail in the day of battle.

Verse 14

Stand therefore. Now follows a description of the arms which they were enjoined to wear. We must not, however, inquire very minutely into the meaning of each word; for an allusion to military customs is all that was intended. Nothing can be more idle than the extraordinary pains which some have taken to discover the reason why righteousness is made a breastplate, instead of a girdle. Paul's design was to touch briefly on the most important points required in a Christian, and to adapt them to the comparison which he had already used.

Truth, which means sincerity of mind, is compared to a girdle. Now, a girdle was, in ancient times, one of the most important parts of military armor. Our attention is thus directed to the fountain of sincerity; for the purity of the gospel ought to remove from our minds all guile, and from our hearts all hypocrisy. Secondly, he recommends righteousness, and desires that it should be a breastplate for protecting the breast. Some imagine that this refers to a freely bestowed righteousness, or the imputation of righteousness, by which pardon of sin is obtained. But such matters ought not, I think, to have been mentioned on the present occasion; for the subject now under discussion is a blameless life. He enjoins us to be adorned, first, with integrity, and next with a devout and holy life.

Verse 15

And your feet shod. The allusion, if I mistake not, is to the military greaves; for they were always reckoned a part of the armor, and were even used for domestic purposes. As soldiers covered their legs and feet to protect them against cold and other injuries, so we must be shod with the gospel, if we would pass unhurt through the world. It is the gospel of peace, and it is so called, as every reader must perceive, from its effects; for it is the message of our reconciliation to God, and nothing else gives peace to the conscience. But what is the meaning of the word preparation? Some explain it as an injunction to be prepared for the gospel; but it is the effect of the gospel which I consider to be likewise expressed by this term. We are enjoined to lay aside every hinderance, and to be prepared both for journey and for war. By nature we dislike exertion, and want agility. A rough road and many other obstacles retard our progress, and we are discouraged by the smallest annoyance. On these accounts, Paul holds out the gospel as the fittest means for undertaking and performing the expedition. Erasmus proposes a circumlocution, (ut sitis parati ,) that ye may be prepared; but this does not appear to convey the true meaning.

Verse 16

Taking the shield of faith. Though faith and the word of God are one, yet Paul assigns to them two distinct offices. I call them one, because the word is the object of faith, and cannot be applied to our use but by faith; as faith again is nothing, and can do nothing, without the word. But Paul, neglecting so subtle a distinction, allowed himself to expatiate at large on the military armor. In the first Epistle to the Thessalonians he gives both to faith and to love the name of a breastplate, — "putting on the breastplate of faith and love," (1 Thessalonians 5:8.) All that was intended, therefore, was obviously this, — "He who possesses the excellencies of character which are here described is protected on every hand."

And yet it is not without reason that the most necessary instruments of warfare — a sword and a shield — are compared to faith, and to the word of God. In the spiritual combat, these two hold the highest rank. By faith we repel all the attacks of the devil, and by the word of God the enemy himself is slain. If the word of God shall have its efficacy upon us through faith, we shall be more than sufficiently armed both for opposing the enemy and for putting him to flight. And what shall we say of those who take from a Christian people the word of God? Do they not rob them of the necessary armor, and leave them to perish without a struggle? There is no man of any rank who is not bound to be a soldier of Christ. But if we enter the field unarmed, if we want our sword, how shall we sustain that character?

Wherewith ye shall be able to quench all the darts. But quench appears not to be the proper word. Why did he not use, instead of it, ward off or shake off, or some such word? Quench is far more expressive; for it is adapted to the epithet applied to darts The darts of Satan are not only sharp and penetrating, but — what makes them more destructive — they are fiery Faith will be found capable, not only of blunting their edge, but of quenching their heat.

"This," says John, "is the victory that overcometh the world, even our faith." (1 John 5:4.)

Verse 17

And take the helmet of salvation. In a passage already quoted, (1 Thessalonians 5:8,) "the hope of salvation" is said to be a helmet, which I consider to be in the same sense as this passage. The head is protected by the best helmet, when, elevated by hope, we look up towards heaven to that salvation which is promised. It is only therefore by becoming the object of hope that salvation is a helmet.

Verse 18

Praying always with all prayer. Having instructed the Ephesians to put on their armor, he now enjoins them to fight by prayer. This is the true method. To call upon God is the chief exercise of faith and hope; and it is in this way that we obtain from God every blessing. Prayer and supplication are not greatly different from each other, except that supplication is only one branch of prayer

With all perseverance. We are exhorted to persevere in prayer. Every tendency to weariness must be counteracted by a cheerful performance of the duty. With unabated ardor we must continue our prayers, though we do not immediately obtain what we desire. If, instead of with all perseverance, some would render it, with all Earnestness, I would have no objection to the change.

But what is the meaning of always? Having already spoken of continued application, does he twice repeat the same thing? I think not. When everything flows on prosperously, — when we are easy and cheerful, we seldom feel any strong excitement to prayer, — or rather, we never flee to God, but when we are driven by some kind of distress. Paul therefore desires us to allow no opportunity to pass, — on no occasion to neglect prayer; so that praying always is the same thing with praying both in prosperity and in adversity.

For all saints. There is not a moment of our life at which the duty of prayer may not be urged by our own wants. But unremitting prayer may likewise be enforced by the consideration, that the necessities of our brethren ought to move our sympathy. And when is it that some members of the church are not suffering distress, and needing our assistance? If, at any time, we are colder or more indifferent about prayer than we ought to be, because we do not feel the pressure of immediate necessity, — let us instantly reflect how many of our brethren are worn out by varied and heavy afflictions, — are weighed down by sore perplexity, or are reduced to the lowest distress. If reflections like these do not rouse us from our lethargy, we must have hearts of stone. But are we to pray for believers only? Though the apostle states the claims of the godly, he does not exclude others. And yet in prayer, as in all other kind offices, our first care unquestionably is due to the saints.

Verse 19

And for me. For himself, in a particular manner, he enjoins the Ephesians to pray. Hence we infer that there is no man so richly endowed with gifts as not to need this kind of assistance from his brethren, so long as he remains in this world. Who will ever be better entitled to plead exemption from this necessity than Paul? Yet he entreats the prayers of his brethren, and not hypocritically, but from an earnest desire of their aid. And what does he wish that they should ask for him? That utterance may be given to me. What then? Was he habitually dumb, or did fear restrain him from making an open profession of the gospel? By no means; but there was reason to fear lest his splendid commencement should not be sustained by his future progress. Besides, his zeal for proclaiming the gospel was so ardent that he was never satisfied with his exertions. And indeed, if we consider the weight and importance of the subject, we shall all acknowledge that we are very far from being able to handle it in a proper manner. Accordingly he adds,

Verse 20

As I ought to speak; meaning, that to proclaim the truth of the gospel as it ought to be proclaimed, is a high and rare attainment. Every word here deserves to be carefully weighed. Twice he uses the expression boldly, — "that I may open my mouth boldly, " "that therein I may speak boldly. " Fear hinders us from preaching Christ openly and fearlessly, while the absence of all restraint and disguise in confessing Christ is demanded from his ministers. Paul does not ask for himself the powers of an acute debater, or, I should rather say, of a dexterous sophist, that he might shield himself from his enemies by false pretences. It is, that I may open my mouth, to make a clear and strong confession; for when the mouth is half shut, the sounds which it utters are doubtful and confused. To open the mouth, therefore, is to speak with perfect freedom, without the smallest dread.

But does not Paul discover unbelief, when he entertains doubts as to his own stedfastness, and implores the intercession of others? No. He does not, like unbelievers, seek a remedy which is contrary to the will of God, or inconsistent with his word. The only aids on which he relies are those which he knows to be sanctioned by the Divine promise and approbation. It is the command of God, that believers shall pray for one another. How consoling then must it be to each of them to learn that the care of his salvation is enjoined on all the rest, and to be informed by God himself that the prayers of others on his behalf are not poured out in vain! Would it be lawful to refuse what the Lord himself has offered? Each believer, no doubt, ought to have been satisfied with the Divine assurance, that as often as he prayed he would be heard. But if, in addition to all the other manifestations of his kindness, God were pleased to declare that he will listen to the prayers of others in our behalf, would it be proper that this bounty should be slighted, or rather, ought we not to embrace it with open arms?

Let us therefore remember that Paul, when he resorted to the intercessions of his brethren, was influenced by no distrust or hesitation. His eagerness to obtain them arose from his resolution that no privilege which the Lord had given him should be overlooked. How absurdly then do Papists conclude from Paul's example, that we ought to pray to the dead! Paul was writing to the Ephesians, to whom he had it in his power to communicate his sentintents. But what intercourse have we with the dead? As well might they argue that we ought to invite angels to our feasts and entertainments, because among men friendship is promoted by such kind offices.

Verse 21

But that, ye also may know. Uncertain or false reports frequently produce uneasiness, chiefly, no doubt, in weak minds, but sometimes also in thoughtful and steady persons. To prevent this danger, Paul sends Tychicus, from whom the Ephesians would receive full information. The holy solicitude which Paul felt about the interests of religion, or, to use his own language, "the care of all the churches," (2 Corinthians 11:28,) was thus strikingly evinced. When death stood constantly before his eyes, neither the dread of death, nor anxiety about himself, prevented him from making provision for the most distant churches. Another man would have said, "My own affairs require all the attention I can give. It would be more reasonable that all should run to my assistance, than that they should expect from me the smallest relief." But Paul acts a different part, and sends in every direction to strengthen the churches which he had founded.

Tychicus is commended, that his statements may be more fully believed. A faithful minister in the Lord. It is not easy to say, whether this refers to the public ministry of the church, or to the private attentions which Paul had received from Tychicus. This uncertainty arises from these two expressions being connected, a beloved brother and faithful minister in the Lord. The former refers to Paul, to whom the second may

126

be supposed also to apply. I am more inclined, however, to understand it as denoting the public ministry; for I do not think it probable that Paul would have sent any man who did not hold such a rank in the church, as would secure the respectful attention of the Ephesians.

Verse 23

Peace be to the brethren. I consider the word peace, as in the salutations of the Epistles, to mean prosperity. Yet if the reader shall prefer to view it as signifying harmony, because, immediately afterwards, Paul mentions love, I do not object to that interpretation, or rather, it agrees better with the context. He wishes the Ephesians to be peaceable and quiet among themselves; and this, he presently adds, may be obtained by brotherly love and by agreement in faith From this prayer we learn that faith and love, as well as peace itself, are gifts of God bestowed upon us through Christ, — that they come equally from God the Father and the Lord Jesus Christ.

Verse 24

Grace be with all. The meaning is, "May God continue to bestow his favor on all who love Jesus Christ with a pure conscience!" The Greek word, which I follow Erasmus in translating sincerity, (ἐν ἀφθαρσίᾳ,) signifies literally uncorruptedness, which deserves attention on account of the beauty of the metaphor. Paul intended to state indirectly, that, when the heart of man is free from all hypocrisy, it will be free from all corruption. This prayer conveys to us the instruction, that the only way of enjoying the light of the Divine countenance is to love sincerely God's own Son, in whom his love toward us has been declared and confirmed. But let there be no hypocrisy; for most men, while they are not unwilling to make some professions of religion, entertain exceedingly low notions of Christ, and worship him with pretended homage. I wish there were not so many instances in the present day to prove that Paul's admonition, to love our Lord Jesus Christ in sincerity is as necessary as ever.

END OF THE COMMENTARIES ON THE EPISTLE TO THE EPHESIANS.

THANK YOU

Thank you for purchasing this book. We truly value your custom. This book was put together to provide you with a collection of good commentary resources on the books of the Bible. It is our prayerful hope that God might use this work for His own glory and sovereign will.

We would be delighted to hear from you and received any messages, suggestions or corrections. You can contact us at:

expansivecommentarycollection@gmail.com

It is our promise that you email address will not be added to any mailing list or used for any purpose other than to communicate regarding this commentary series.

We trust that the Lord will continue to bless you as you live for Him.

Printed in Great Britain
by Amazon

14984188R00078